QUESTIONS
SCHOOL
GOVERNORS ASK

Also by Joan Sallis:

BASICS FOR SCHOOL GOVERNORS

QUESTIONS SCHOOL GOVERNORS ASK

JOAN SALLIS

NETWORK**EDUCATIONAL**PRESS

THE TIMES EDUCATIONAL SUPPLEMENT

Published by Network Educational Press Ltd
PO Box 635
Stafford
ST16 1BF

Published 2004

ISBN 1 85539 146 5

Managing Editor – Anne Oppenheimer
Layout – Neil Hawkins, NEP

Printed in Great Britain by
MPG Books Ltd, Bodmin, Cornwall

Contents

Foreword

This is the third selection of questions and answers to be published since I was first asked to write the 'Agenda' feature in the *Times Educational Supplement* fourteen years or so ago. It covers the years 1998 to 2003 inclusive and I have chosen the themes which occur most often, but adding a few less common questions which seemed to me to be of lasting interest.

Despite changes in the emphasis of government education policies and regulations, a few themes remain remarkably constant over the years. The third section, 'The Head Teacher and the Governing Body', is the longest and there was enough material for half as much again. Indeed selection on this subject was quite difficult, but then, as we all know, it is a relationship which, good or bad, is the main influence on the quality of the work. Close behind is the final section, 'Working Together', which includes procedures, relationships with the chair, the resolution of difficult issues, and, of course, becoming a good team. Section 1, 'Roles and Boundaries', covers a wide range of territorial disputes which make the border between governance and management a perennial source of incidents, while Section 2, 'Problems of Representing Others', illustrates how difficult every group on the governing body, but particularly parents, find it to balance constituency expectations with the needs of the school. The relevance of these four main areas of concern is likely to continue as succeeding generations confront the same problems.

The period covered in this collection includes the impact of two major Labour Education Acts – the School Framework and Standards Act of 1998 and the Education Act 2002. This left me with some problems about editing the material – the answers rather than the questions – where new law had a bearing. I decided in the end that I had to bring these up to date, since the alternatives were either to mislead present-day readers or to accept a rash of footnotes. This means that at the time of writing the information given or assumed on law and regulations is accurate.

The two Labour Education Acts followed a brief period of calm after the spate of legislation in the 1980s and early 1990s which shaped the present structures. There have also been marked changes in the emphasis of government rhetoric on education in the New Labour years, changes which have left many governors who thought they knew where they stood politically in some turmoil. Nevertheless the majority of governors who ask me questions are still concerned with the handful of unchangeables represented in the main sections of this book – their role and its limits, their problems in representing particular interest groups, their relations with the head teacher and staff, the efficiency of their working arrangements and the interplay of different interests within the governing body. These remain the big issues with succeeding generations, and it often amazes me that their questions betray so little of the great ideological tensions which allegedly dominate the education debate of the day – tensions between equality and diversity, specialisation and equality, equality and choice, not to mention turmoil in the examination system and endless argument about standards. One can only conclude that despite all the rhetoric these issues seem to intrude less into the debates going on in real schools than politicians might imagine.

What does come through in almost all the questions is a deep and increasing commitment to this form of public service and to the education system itself; a concern for fairness in meeting the needs of all children and especially those whose needs are greatest; a strong sense of responsibility to parents and the community; and a passion for openness, fair dealing and equality within the work of the governing body. In particular I am astonished – and heads might do worse than ponder this – by the way in which values which used to be considered the preserve of education professionals have spread into the wider school community of parents and governors, particularly the concern for special educational needs. This is surely a source of great strength to schools, especially in leafy areas known to all where at one time a meeting on special needs, to be well-attended, would have to be called 'Are slow learners holding your child back?'! It seems that a healthy majority now understand that success in schooling is indivisible, and this is what being a governor has taught new generations of 'outsiders' and those with whom they come in contact.

Of course I have met many thousands of these people over the years as well as receiving their letters. I can only say that they remain an inspiration which illuminates every day. My thanks to the *TES* for this privileged contact and for their support, and to Network Educational Press for bringing you this collection.

Joan Sallis
February 2004

Part One:

Roles and Boundaries

Probably the subject most frequently raised by governors is that of territory. What are school governors for? How do they fit into the life of a school, and where is the boundary between their work and that of the head and professional staff? Where are the lines they mustn't cross and how will they know if they've crossed them? I don't pretend it's easy to find words to illuminate these boundaries, and I try almost daily to find pictures to offer instead. It's crucially important to help both governors and professionals to see their roles clearly, since demarcation disputes embitter relationships and impede the work of essentially well-motivated people.

It does help to start with a definition of a head teacher's job, and also to have illustrations from other more concrete activities. For instance it would be a good start if governors understood that the head has authority to deploy the school's resources of space, staff, equipment and time – within the broad framework set by the governing body – to meet the day-by-day learning needs of the school; to create an orderly environment for that learning; and deal with threats to that order as they arise. The quality of teaching and the development of teachers is also head teachers' territory (as their name suggests) and so is routine communication on the school's behalf with other agencies. Understanding this alone is enough to prevent many new governors' 'transgressions' brought to my attention. I am thinking particularly of well-meaning parent governors who take it upon themselves to visit that teacher whose class all the parents are saying is out of control; who might when visiting a class challenge the punishment meted out in their view unfairly to a child; or who might suggest to the head that a certain teacher needs more in-service training.

Many of these problems involve not only better understanding of the boundaries but also the vital recognition that an *individual* governor has no authority to challenge or change anything, even if the matter in question is within the governing body's territory and even if it is in itself a wholly sensible intervention. Perhaps this should be emphasised even more in governor training: lapses not only damage the relationship with the head but often upset individual teachers. Delicacy is even needed when seeing a teacher about one's own child, because a less confident teacher may be too ready to think one is 'pulling rank'.

As for illustrations from other activities, I keep trying to find better ones. One which seems to get across comes from a sad time in our family life. It was a project to create a memorial garden for babies who died at or near birth. A local authority donated the land, a newly bereaved father who was a professional landscaper joined the group in the nick of time, but a lot of money still had to be raised to ensure that the garden survived to comfort generations of parents long after its founders were forgotten. I thought a lot about the trustees accepting that responsibility for generations to come. They wouldn't expect to cut the grass, prune the shrubs or choose new plants, or interfere with those for whom such care would be a day-by-day responsibility, and there would be money to pay trained people. But it would be their responsibility to protect the vision of those who founded the garden, to keep a watchful eye on its overall design and the health and balance of its plants through the changing seasons, and to distribute the funds raised for that purpose wisely to honour the babies remembered there and their parents.

Another picture is the board of a shipping company, because its members could less easily drop in now and then and get into trouble with the captain for interfering! They wouldn't order the crew about, decide how to punish a sailor drunk on duty, fuel the boilers or check the lifebelts. But they *would* take an interest in crew morale and the factors influencing it. They *would* draw up guidelines for behaviour and sanctions, and take a broad view on fuel economy. Above all they wouldn't check the lifebelts, but they *would* make sure there were systems in place to ensure appropriate and regular checks. *Inventing or endorsing systems to make things happen or stop things happening can be a major governing body job.*

Most cases of provocative intrusion arise not from *governing body* error but from enthusiastic beginners who believe that they can somehow or other put things right on their own. We can't say often enough that only the governing body, acting within the rules and by majority vote if necessary, can change anything. Nevertheless I would be the last person to imply that all conflicts over territory arise from inappropriate behaviour by governors, innocent or otherwise. I observe that a few heads draw the lines in their own favour in ways the law would not always support, and have never in their hearts accepted the role successive governments have given to school governing bodies. Many more will accept governors' role but overreact to well-meaning if ill-judged infringements. Those who provide leadership training for current and aspiring head teachers have a big responsibility to win acceptance of the role of the governing body as an agent of accountability for a vital public service. Like Parliament, local councils, trusts of all kinds, the magistracy and the jury, it is part of a society which holds lay bodies accountable to the public for the probity and efficiency of those who serve its needs. But too often trainers themselves belong to a professional tradition which is reluctant to accept this, much less communicate it to succeeding generations. The result in schools is a battle for ascendancy which takes a lot of energy away from children's learning.

What does 'supporting the school' really mean?

I am a governor as well as working with governors in a local authority, and I wrestle a lot with the word 'support', so often used, so much misused, by heads as well as governors. If you ask either what the main role of governors is, you as often as not get the answer 'to support the school' and although there is a sense in which it is the only right answer, it worries me because it is so often used to justify attitudes which I find distasteful. Heads use it to get their own way or deal with governors who are too challenging for their liking, governors use it to excuse cowardice in tackling things they know to be wrong or to cover up the fact that they haven't really a clue about what they are doing but like to feel good. Is it really a definable word, do you think, or should we drop it?

Answer

I know exactly what you mean and you put it very well. It isn't just in the governor world either, but among governors it can be pretty dangerous. So for a start, is there any need to say it? Why would anybody in their senses take on all that unpaid work and far more kicks than ha'pence if they didn't want to give something, either to a particular school which plays or has played a part in their lives, or more generally to support – here we go – an activity about which they feel passionately? Yes, all right, maybe there are a few who think it gives them a sense of importance which life has otherwise withheld, but these don't in my experience last long. I don't meet them often now.

I take it you are asking me to unpick the word a bit to help all those who guide and counsel governors? So are we just cheerleaders, and if we are not do we have to be called interfering busybodies? A tall order, that. I think you just have to say that if it means you wish the best for this school, speak well of it outside, want it to make the sort of decisions which will enable it to flourish and go on improving, and stand by it through difficulties which, despite those good decisions, sometimes happen, and even occasionally those which its own folly has brought upon it, then yes, you are there to support the school. Just as you hope you do your family and friends, in fact. But the governing body – as distinct from the individual governor – is also the agent, for a wide range of interests, of the school's accountability to the public, and it certainly isn't going to be possible for that body always to say everything about the way it is managed is right, all the time, or put up with 'otherwise you're not my friend' talk. Challenge has to be part of the support, otherwise it's not worth having, and in that sense yes, I suppose I can live with the word both in governors' work and the individual relationships where it is often similarly misused.

I feel just as ambivalent about that 'critical friend' label invented by the government. Yes, I know your friend is the one who loves you so much she can tell you that red doesn't suit you, or you're putting on weight, but nobody told 350,000 governors that it was the governing body, not the individual, who had that role. I imagine all these people lying sleepless, trying to think of something critical to say tomorrow when they visit the school. And what school needs between nine and twenty (new GB sizes, folks) critical friends, all saying something different?

> Two things I'm sure about. One is that you can't create lasting school improvement just by being nasty, and the other that you don't produce failure simply by being too nice!

Can you help us heal this rift?

Until this last Spring term when the funding crisis affecting many schools hit us for six, this governing body of a large comprehensive worked reasonably well. We were badly affected by the budget cut for 2003–4 and it was soon clear that there was no hope of rescue by the LEA or anyone else. The trouble was that instead of a useful carry-over (which we had managed for many years, and would have done again if the head teacher had not set her heart on some ambitious new policies), we had a deficit.

The head was only appointed eighteen months or so ago and had what some governors thought was a mistaken desire to develop two new subjects, drama and media studies, as options, believing they would attract more and brighter students. This divided the governing body at the time and the small number who were against it never forgave the rest. But with majority support, including mine from the chair, we appointed two new staff and equipment was purchased and modest building conversions made. Now with cuts, and stuck with these costs, we had nowhere to turn. Several older staff who were already talking early retirement volunteered for redundancy. We made some other economies and have got by.

The new departments are thriving, with very large groups. But the staff who left were popular with our older governors who had opposed the changes, and these have refused to forgive and forget, blaming the head for all our problems and, I have to say, being very uncooperative. The atmosphere is bad. Reading what you said about the meaning of 'support' in last week's 'Agenda', I realise that the head does expect support as a right, and doesn't feel it is up to her to mend matters. Can you help both of us? She knows I am writing.

Answer

Support is not a right if by that your head means unquestioning endorsement by every governor. *Individual* governors are not obliged to support everything put before them, but the *governing body* is obliged to support the decisions of its majority. Your head will have to learn to live with different opinions, and dissenters on the governing body must understand that although they are entitled to their opinions, once a decision is made they must accept majority views and do their best for the school in whatever situation it finds itself. I assume three things. Firstly, that a majority backed the changes, which were certainly such as to require governing body approval. Secondly, that you have overcome the financial crisis and that the redundancies were genuinely voluntary. Thirdly, that the new options have revitalised the curriculum. If all these assumptions are correct I think you are justified as chair in pointing this out to dissenters and asking for their co-operation now in building pride in the school. As for the head, she is justified in feeling a bit sore about all the backtracking, especially as she could not have forecast this year's financial shocks. All the same, she cannot expect every controversial change to go through without dissent. She may need to listen rather more carefully to opposing views, and also feel more of an obligation to make the case for what she wants to do. These two things often make a big difference to how people accept that they have lost an argument. They do not then feel that their support has been taken for granted. It never should be. If you and your head could agree on this you have the basis for an agenda item reviewing the curriculum changes and the restoration of solvency, and asking for unity based on majority opinion.

The most impressive governors I have met up and down the country include many who have started with no specialised knowledge or experience but with a tremendous commitment to the job and a seemingly natural empathy with schools and teachers. They tend to learn very fast, but retain a purity of understanding which you sometimes feel too much knowledge might compromise.

A 'special interest' governor makes waves

Each governor in our school has a special subject – mine is maths – and I believe this specialisation is government policy. We have to monitor school effectiveness, and I do have a qualification in maths. I have sat in on classes and made helpful suggestions. I have asked for the schemes of work and spent hours studying them and again commented where I could. We take a few subjects at a time at governors' meetings but I also mention anything of particular interest as it arises. Now one teacher has become very touchy and has complained that I am interfering and criticising her, and she has refused to let me observe her classes. She is inexperienced and I did suggest some better approaches which she could try. What do you advise?

Answer

There is a lot of misunderstanding about these 'specialisations' by governors and sometimes I think they are more trouble then they are worth. First of all, apart from one or two areas – ESN for instance – where the government does recommend or require a special governor, it is *not* a government requirement to have these attachments across the board, though many governing bodies do introduce them as a means of providing a focus for individual members to learn about the school and as a way of increasing the knowledge base of the governing body as a whole. In this sense they are worthwhile, but they need a tremendous amount of care, and probably account for more upset governors and teachers who write to me than anything else.

Let me say again, a subject attachment gives a 'window' on the school through which an individual governor can become familiar with how children learn. *This is governor training rather than performance monitoring*. Such a focus is, I suppose, helpful to some, though I myself would much prefer a month of duty or an attachment to a class as a link. Subject attachment is also said to provide a way in which a whole governing body improves its knowledge of the curriculum, but I am less sure about this. But in both cases the aim is to learn, not judge, and this should be made absolutely clear to both governors and teachers. If a governor has some training in the subject it may be even more dangerous, because less confident teachers will see it as inspection, interpreting the most innocent remark as criticism.

Yes, observe classes. Show interest and appreciation. Yes, look at schemes of work and other relevant material, but always make it clear that you are the one who is learning, not the teacher. Any reports to the governing body should be general, positive, and never include criticism of individual teachers. That is not our job, either as individuals or as a body. I know I have to say this often, but the governing body is not there to manage teachers or teaching. It is there to provide the best possible environment for teaching and learning, to establish a framework of policy and principle within which teachers can work effectively, to establish sound and equitable systems for that work to be checked, encouraged and further developed. It is the job of professionals – subject leaders and ultimately the head teacher – to check the work of individual teachers, to advise them and develop their skills. In any case, even the jobs which properly belong to governors are only theirs corporately. An individual governor has no power to act alone, no power to change anything. This well-meaning governor should apologise to teachers she has upset, and make it clear that she knows that her visits are to make her a better governor, not the teacher a better teacher.

Knowledge conveys privilege, and if there are some governors who sit there and think 'That doesn't sound right to me but I'd better keep quiet because I don't know where it says that', they are immediately excluded from a decision they should be sharing.

A new governor in trouble

I have only been a governor a couple of months, having been elected early in the Autumn term. I thought I was doing the right thing but it seems I have already upset the head and one of the teachers, which was a shock because I have always been very supportive of the school in the Friends Association. We were having a post-mortem on the exam results in the curriculum committee, and I asked why one form had done so much worse in geography than the rest of the year. I knew that geography was taught in mixed ability classes. I had picked this up from parents in that year who had given me the details. The head answered that there were differences in ability between groups even though they were theoretically a random mix, and this had always been a difficult form, which had also had a change of tutor during the year. Afterwards the head told me that I should not have implied criticism of a teacher in that way and the teacher herself tackled me and was really furious. I didn't mention her or mean it personally at all and I know now that she has been ill, but was I really speaking out of turn?

Answer

I think that in your first term it might have been more tactful to ask the head your question in private, or sound out your chair on the point first, because it was predictable that it would have become personalised, even though I'm sure you will always be careful never to mention a teacher by name at a meeting in any critical context. On the other hand it is the sort of question which individual governors do ask on this sort of occasion in a committee, and parents ask them among themselves all the time. I think it's a pity that there's such a tradition of pretending that all teachers are equally successful, and I wish we could be a bit more relaxed about the differences. But was your question proper? Well, the governing body is charged to promote school improvement and it's appropriate to ask for information about unexplained differences in outcomes, always being careful not to personalise them, but it can easily slip over into personalities if we are not very careful. It is also clearly the head's responsibility, not ours, to take action on individual teacher performance. Indeed I'm sure he will have already noted the point you made. That is why I think it would have been wise to talk to your committee chair first, remembering also that we have no authority as individuals and that there may have been some history you should know. One of the factors which would have upset the teacher is that you could presumably not have got the information from the published data, so it was obviously parents' chatter which lay behind your question. She will be particularly sensitive to criticism if she has been ill, and you weren't to know that.

I'm sure you will have told the teacher that you had not meant your comment personally and that you have now been told that this was a difficult form. But I hope that your fellow governors will still think it right to ask questions when there is a suggestion that any group may be underperforming – after all, there can be many reasons, and some of them *are* within our responsibilities, even if dealing with poor teachers is not.

> A meeting to which some governors were not invited is not a governing body meeting and has no authority… Only the whole governing body has any legal status. Any other meetings are only glorified gossip. I know very well that there are times when governors feel they need to discuss matters which are difficult to bring up with staff present, but we just have to grow up and learn to do it.

Our school is light years behind

The schools you write about may have problems which they consider serious, but to me they come from another world. I would love a meeting which went on too long or where a head talked everybody into the ground. I would relish an argument about whether governors were entitled to know the school's test results or interview candidates for jobs, even if I lost. Our names are listed in the annual report to parents, which the head writes. We sit silently through formal occasions. A new governor caused a diplomatic incident by asking to tour the school in session to 'get a feel for it'. None of us ever enters between meetings, and the meetings are hardly worth taking your coat off for. When 'Agenda' suggests something like the head extending his report to look into the future (we get a gabbled five-minute account of school events read from a notebook and not punctuated, never mind circulated) I wonder if it's the same country. Staff governors never open their mouths. Parent governors wouldn't dream of raising an issue, although they get many complaints. You can settle an argument or heal a breach, but unless you can raise the dead, don't bother coming here.

Answer

I am glad you wrote. I'm sorry if 'Agenda' seems like fairyland, but I can only answer questions I'm asked and I am very glad to have yours. I do know that there are dark places like yours in the system. I salute your courage to keep going and to write with such vigour. It's hard, but if you stick together and choose your ground you can achieve some movement, I'm sure. Remember any three governors can call a special meeting – it can't be refused. Could you ask to have one on 'Governors and their role'? Go armed with plenty of material and suggestions, not too wild, and ask if you can have someone from your governor support services in the LEA to attend, to guide you in making your role more real. Your letter suggests you have plenty of material on good practice.

Remember the Education Act of 2002 says 'the conduct of the school shall be under the general direction of the governing body'. This is the law of the land, and you have the right to say you would like to make a reality of those words. Make it clear that you know there are boundaries and that you will honour them, never crossing the line between strategic policy and day-by-day management. At best your head will change slowly, and creating fear of territorial warfare will not help the process. Keep your requests for information and consultation very simple and concrete to start, the sort of things you would like to know about the operation of the school to equip you to play your part in the policies and programmes the law clearly intends should be subject to your consent.

You may need some help from your LEA, who could perhaps provide a rough programme to show the sort of subjects on which a typical school of your size would need to arrange consultation on each term, or even invite another head to run through his or her governors' programme. The LEA should make sure yours knows that many schools also have regular opportunities for governors to see the school at work. I don't understand how LEAs let heads go on in this way, but they *must* accept that you have a right to ask their help to get things on a better footing. Many governor support teams indeed provide team-building sessions at the school for a school with problems.

> Challenge has to be part of the support, otherwise neither is worth having.

Reacting to the exam results

I am a parent governor of a city comprehensive. It is not easy for a school like ours to get GCSE results to be proud of, but we understand all the problems and don't expect miracles. This year, however, the percentage of A to C grades is the worst in our history, and we have already this week had an informal meeting of those governors who were contactable in a member's house to talk about what our approach should be. Unfortunately the head heard about it, and this weekend, the last of the holiday, was very angry, because she felt it was a hostile gesture and that it was wrong to meet when we could not include her or the teacher governors. It was true we couldn't reach them, but to be honest we would have found it hard to react to the news frankly in their presence and we wanted to discuss how we should handle it. They are so defensive, you see, and the trouble is that in past years the head and staff have resisted any request for a 'post-mortem' and refused to allow any kind of involvement of governors in the review which they must themselves be planning. We are very supportive of the school but as representatives we feel we must be in the picture and able to respond to questions.

Answer

I understand, but I am sorry you felt you had to meet unofficially as a restricted group of governors, because it perpetuates the 'them and us' situation you seem to be in. I know yours isn't the usual boundary dispute which governor guidance deals with, but it is about one very important principle, namely that only the whole governing body has a role and its power is indivisible. To me there is no acceptable half-way house between a moan to a colleague you happen to meet in the supermarket – which may be wrong but is natural – and a special governors' meeting of which *all* governors are informed. Even if you had been able to arrange the latter it would still have been taken as divisive because you suspected that not all the staff concerned would be back. I personally believe that unofficial meetings of selected governors in people's homes should be avoided in all but dire situations: all my experience is that they lead to a divided and dysfunctional governing body which risks losing its moral right to participate.

Having said this, it is quite unacceptable that the governing body is not encouraged to discuss exam results within the school with staff members, and indeed other staff outside the governing body who have a role, and to do so at the first reasonable opportunity. I know how hard a post-mortem can be for teachers in a school like yours. They often work twice as hard to achieve half as much as others, but it is the law that school results are not only made public but specifically reported to parents, and it is also the governing body's responsibility to achieve school improvement. The logic is that governors know the background and the school's views of the reasons for changes in either direction, so that they can answer questions sensibly and indeed put the best construction on the published figures if there is justification for it.

Your role could be a wholly constructive one if you were not forced to react to bad news in a divisive way and without the benefit of informed analysis. I think your chair should apologise to the head for the private meeting and accept that it was unwise, but make strongly the case for a full meeting as soon as possible to review the results. If staff remain obdurate you may have to ask the LEA for help.

A market-researcher out of control

One of our co-opted governors is causing great concern, especially among staff. I am a teacher at the school and although I am not a governor I am all too aware of what is going on. This lady works in market research and perhaps this explains her approach, but although she has only been with us less than a year she is going round asking teachers, office staff, even midday supervisors what they think about the school, not to mention parents at the gate and pupils. I understand she has not yet said anything about this at a governors' meeting, though no doubt she will come out with some startling conclusions before long. Some teachers feel that they are being spied upon, others are worried about the use to which she will put the comments they make and perhaps do the school damage. Do you think it is right? I don't think the head is aware of this – perhaps we should ask her to speak to this governor?

Answer

It isn't the first time I've heard this one but it is a more extreme case than most. The busy governor problem at its worst, in fact. No, of course I don't think it is right. I'm all for opinion surveys from time to time, provided they are well-structured and properly managed and above all under the auspices of the *governing body* with the head's agreement. A certain amount of careful listening is part of the role of governors, especially elected ones, parents for instance, since they may need to provide colleagues with some idea of feeling in the 'constituency'. But individuals should never be beavering away on their own with clipboards and leading questions. It is for the governing body as a whole to decide whether and when to use opinion surveys and what use should be made of the results.

I'm surprised a teacher or support staff governor has not reacted to this by now, since it is an issue for the governing body. I don't think the head is the right person to complain to, however. As I often say, it isn't for the head to tell governors how to behave. If he or she has heard about this – and I'd be surprised if s/he didn't know it was going on – the proper thing is to have a word with the chair. The governing body must provide its own discipline, and the chair is the obvious source of this in the first instance, though at some stage if his or her tactful approach is not acted upon it may have to come up to the full governing body.

Probably innocence and lack of experience, combined with the governor's professional leaning, lie behind this action, but in the unlikely event of its not being soluble without a fuss, there is a procedure which you will find in detail in your Guide to the Law for a governing body to remove a co-opted governor. (Parent and teacher governors are not covered because they are elected, and foundation and LEA governors can only be removed by their appointing body.) It is quite rigorous – rightly so – and full of safeguards for natural justice. It takes place over two meetings, and of course the person must know what is alleged and have a chance to reply, accompanied by a friend if he or she wants. There is also a new procedure, in regulations made under the 2002 Act, and operating from September 2003, for suspending for one year any governor whose actions have brought the governing body into disrepute. I don't altogether like this, partly because it might be used for a governor who with good reason wants to open things up, partly because there is no suggestion for follow-up action. Some LEAs are urging governors to keep it for really bad cases. I'm sure yours won't require such drastic measures.

How to go wrong on a school visit

I am not inexperienced. But until recently, mainly because of the attitudes of key players shall I say, we never visited the school except for meetings or exclusion appeals. Only getting a new chair and a new head at the same time have opened a few things up. One result is I was made governor for literacy (I am sympathetic as my daughter has slight dyslexia) and made my first visit, hoping later to observe some classes. The teacher with this responsibility seemed uneasy from the outset, and when I asked to see the materials used and records showing improvement over a period, she became defensive and said these were professional records and I was not qualified to judge results. I left it there, thinking she might come round, mentioned it to the head (who is very open and clearly had a word) and the records were produced. The boys had improved much less than the girls (indeed hardly at all) with intensive help. Mentioning this clearly touched a raw spot, so much so that I could not pursue it. Next time unfortunately I had to raise a concern about my own daughter who is on a different programme and the teacher remarked sharply that governors' children didn't get special treatment. Should I feel angry or inadequate?

Answer

I am glad to hear your school has become more open, if rather suddenly. Contact with children at work gives reality to so many of the decisions we have to make. Your head perhaps embarked on the new regime with insufficient preparation of staff or discussion with governors about ground-rules. I know that you have acted in good faith, and with luck and a little more scene-setting your role could have been an instant success. One of the reasons I've always been doubtful about subject attachments is that the governor could appear from the outset as some kind of rival specialist (and often will in practice be someone who does have special knowledge or, like you, a personal interest – natural but dangerous). It comes very near those lines which we cross at our peril. Teachers must understand that we come to learn, not inspect, and also that an individual governor has no power, so is no threat. The occasional teacher will be very insecure, and this must be allowed for. My other concern is that an attached governor shouldn't allow other governors to duck the responsibility, particularly for special needs.

With hindsight, quiet observation of a class or two (with the head's help to put it in context and pave the way) might have been a better if less logical start than seeing plans and records, because you could have established your goodwill and genuine interest. You might have thought to say how much help your daughter had received (i.e. before you had a problem!) and what hard work it was with boys despite her efforts to differentiate appropriately, if there was evidence of that.

14

Later, when a governors' agenda had the subject listed, you could have asked for some help interpreting the progress charts they would be sure to get beforehand. And when you had a problem with your own child you should have been careful to make clear that you weren't there as a governor (or got your partner to do it). You may think this pussyfoot and ask why teachers have to be so touchy, but many don't know a lot about governors and your appearance did represent a very sudden policy change. Preparing the ground (with the head's help) and advancing carefully are the answers.

The doghouse isn't the best place to spend the night.

Another unofficial meeting

Our most recent Key Stage 2 results were very poor and our successes in the 11+, which we still have in our area, well down on previous years. Parents are naturally upset. It will affect the school's reputation locally, its numbers and therefore its budget. (We parent governors all think the new teacher allocated to Year 6 as soon as she was appointed is the cause.) A parent governor agreed to host an unofficial meeting to discuss this but of course we didn't invite the head or the teacher governors because we wanted a frank exchange and anyway it took place in the holiday. When the head came back from his holiday he got to hear and was furious. He is a governor and says we had no right to meet like this and also questioned our saying we were responsible for school standards and the quality of the teaching. Worst of all he heard that we voted to assign this new teacher to a lower class, which he said was out of order. He knows I am writing to you for a ruling. We meant well.

Answer

Oh dear. You couldn't legally vote to change a teacher's placing, (a) because governors don't control the way staff (or time, space or equipment) are used in the school (that's the head's management role) and (b) because a meeting to which some governors were not invited is not a governing body meeting and has no authority. Yes, the governing body is responsible for standards and can properly advise on measures to raise them, though the head is the one to take steps to improve individual teachers' performance as well as assigning them to classes. But the real point is not where responsibility lies but the calling of a meeting without the head and staff governors, which is extremely unwise and indeed improper.

Only the whole governing body has any legal status. Any other meetings are only glorified gossip. I know very well that there are times when governors feel they need to discuss matters which are difficult to bring up with staff present, but we just have to grow up and learn to do it. So often when I have been asked to help a governing body in serious difficulties the problem goes back to the habit of working in factions. Firstly there's no future in it, because without the staff's co-operation you can't change anything. Secondly it's wrong because all governors have equal status. Even if the head were not a governor (as you know, they can choose) there is a clear legal right to attend all meetings of the governing body and its committees. But yours is a governor, and so are three school staff. Imagine how you would feel if, because, say, you held views which did not accord with those of your colleagues, they called a meeting without telling you. The end of the road is dominance by cliques. Don't do it. Indeed I think your chair should apologise and I'm sure your head will forget the incident. He'll know it's not an easy job and we all make mistakes.

I'm not saying drop the issue of the poor showing in the last school year, of course. But you cannot in the nature of things be sure you know the reasons – the ability of that intake may have been unusual or there may have been other changes or circumstances besides the change of teacher. Make sure you have a proper comparison taking into account all relevant factors – do you all see your LEA's PANDA (Performance and Assessment) reports? I am sure you will have an honest and positive outcome. After all, you are all on the same side.

How can we deal with a misbehaving governor?

Let me say straight away that I'm not the chairman or the head, just an ordinary governor, and that our head is being very tolerant in the face of extreme provocation by a new parent governor. I believe strongly in governors having a say, heads being accountable, and governors working as a team, and on all counts we were doing well. I am really upset to think that this new governor is going to give us all a bad name. She started by standing at the gate questioning parents on their opinions of the school. Now she talks of distributing a questionnaire in the summer seeking parents' views on the curriculum, the uniform, school rules, even the quality of the teachers. She's also said she will call a general parents' meeting to discuss the findings. We've all been too stunned to respond, but I find I don't know whose job it is to put her straight or how to do it. She's been heard to say that we are a timid and ineffective bunch.

Answer

I will assume you are *not* ineffective, and that your head is one of those rare people who is mature enough to take a new governor's well-meaning excesses in her stride, in which case you are very lucky and owe it to her to help incorporate your new colleague without damage. I also assume that there is no seething pot of parent unrest just waiting for the lid to be lifted: if there were you would bear some responsibility. I would guess that the new governor is hard working and enthusiastic and will be a great colleague once she learns how to work within the team. No one has told her (a) that no governor acting alone has any authority at all and (b) that even when that is accepted there are areas where governors' have no authority, like teacher quality.

But it *is* tricky. Whoever speaks to her – and it could be your chair or an experienced parent governor, in the framework of a welcome-to-the-team meeting, not a reprimand – needs to leave her feeling wanted and motivated, not rejected, so you probably have to live with what she has already done and hope that you can dissuade or divert her from further indiscretions. If you opt for dissuading, start by accepting that it is right for parent governors *as a group* to want to represent parents effectively. But she must also understand that individual governors don't work in isolation and that her approach may not be the most effective way to bring parent concerns to the governing body. Your spokesperson must also say something about the framework within which governors corporately work, and demonstrate that if there were any widespread parent concern about some school policy or practice it could be put on the agenda and thoroughly aired. An example or two about parent concerns which *have* been satisfactorily dealt with in this way would be worth an hour of preaching, and it would be helpful to include also examples of strategic decisions designed to improve the school's performance. (If you can't think of such examples you need to ask why.)

But dissuasion *is* a hazardous option, and diversion could be better. You must have your annual meeting with parents some time in the next seven or eight months. Couldn't your chair convince this new governor that you have there a potentially superb *legal* means of increasing parental influence which sadly has been little exploited, perhaps because the focus has been on reporting about the past rather than flagging future needs and issues which parents could influence? Might your parent governors as a group perhaps be asked to consider how this change of focus could be achieved and to that end form themselves into a planning/editorial group for the report and the meeting? Or is there a similar issue or event where they could take a lead?

I can't support this teacher's promotion

When I became a parent governor I admit that one of the reasons was to keep an eye on what happened to my child in school and look after her interests. There is one teacher who has a bad reputation with parents and is thought to have favourites and to pick on others. I have definitely found this to be true and my own daughter was one of the victims. I tried to get her moved to another class but without success. Now I hear that when our deputy head retires this teacher intends to apply for the post and I might well be asked to be on the panel. Should I accept if asked? Part of me wants to be sure he does not get the job. But the head knows how I feel and might make trouble for me. If I am not elected should I warn those who are, especially if they are not parents?

Answer

Your letter made me rather sad because one of the accusations which damages the standing of parent governors – and I fought hard to have them included when I was young – is that they are too concerned about their own children and can't take a broader view. I think there are very, very few who merit that charge. Of course *as parents* we must all fight for our own children's fair treatment – or better still, if we are governors, get our partner to do so, in order to keep things separate – but governors are there to look after the interests of all children who will attend the school, even those not there yet. It would be wiser if you did not accept a suggestion that you take part, because the regulations say that we should stand aside from any decision if there is any circumstance which makes it hard for us to be impartial. I certainly don't think you should say anything to prejudice those who do take part either, not only because it could get you into legal trouble now but also because any candidate who had a grievance might contest the appointment, with possible serious consequences. Remember that if the teacher concerned does have a reputation for not being fair, the head will certainly not be unaware of it, and he will have a considerable say.

When members fail to do what they've undertaken, NOTICE IT. A little tough love is good for everybody. It involves a totally different conception of what 'voluntary' means. Too often it is an excuse for all the ways in which we fall short. The fact that we can leave when we like, and be replaced by someone really caring and hard-working, should be seen instead as a very powerful reason for the highest standards. Only this can make being a school governor a proud calling.

Should we be involved in applying for specialist status?

Our head and staff have decided to make application for specialist status and are preparing the bid. Is it right that the governing body was never consulted, only informed?

Answer

Certainly not. If ever there was a strategic decision, that to apply for specialist status must surely be one. It changes the character of the school very radically, it commits you to major extensions of the curriculum, may affect your admissions policy, your standing in the community and your spending. Anyway, the school will have to raise considerable sums in sponsorship to apply at all, and I would be surprised if the governors were not expected to help with this, if nothing else. It sounds as if your standing is not really accepted by the head and senior staff and I can only hope that there will be a full discussion with you before the bid goes in at the very least – in fact I don't see how the school can go ahead without your sanction, even if belated. Don't you think you need to discuss the wider questions of your role with the head?

Some conciliatory words all round would be better.

A parent governor oversteps the mark

I have been a hard-working governor but I'm afraid I've blotted my copybook seriously, though I think everyone has overreacted. I help in Class 2 once a week – I'm careful to avoid my children's classes – and I thought the teacher appreciated me and we got on fine. However, she has been a bit stressed recently over marital problems (so it's said). She is sharp with the children and has really overstepped the mark with correcting them. I can usually bite my tongue and busy myself out of her way, but last week she took a little boy's part in the Christmas play (which she produces) away from him because he was persistently annoying the girl in front by twisting her hair and untying her ribbon. I had to speak up for him because he was so terribly upset, but I waited till the end of the lesson and then said I thought it was a ridiculously hard punishment for childish pranks and she shouldn't take out her domestic frustrations on the children. She went berserk and reported it to the head who has asked me to resign since I 'clearly can't keep out of professional matters'. Surely parent governors represent local families and must see that teachers behave professionally with the children and give only fair punishments? Must I resign?

19

Answer

It is not for the head to seek your resignation, and indeed if we are talking formalities it is not all that easy to get rid of an elected (as distinct from a co-opted) governor in any circumstances except for non-attendance or breaking the law. It is also for the governing body as a whole (maybe through the chair) to ensure that members behave appropriately, and suspension for a year is possible in extreme cases. But that is not really the point – you *have* behaved inappropriately, and although not formally correct, the reactions of the head were very understandable, particularly as you were unwise enough to attribute the teacher's hasty action to personal problems – you know how we all hate that! Yes, of course I think the punishment excessive and I hope the boy's parents say so, but I suspect that if you had not intervened the decision would have been reconsidered before the end of the day, certainly if it got to the head's ears. The head will know that this teacher is behaving uncharacteristically and will be dealing with the matter in her own way, I'm sure. But it is not our job as governors to correct teachers or question their actions – managing teachers' performance and conduct is the head's job, and even helping in the class doesn't give an individual governor any right to interfere. But the governing body as a whole does have a responsibility to formulate pupil behaviour guidelines in a policy which will guide staff in day-by-day decisions, and such a policy could very well include something about appropriate sanctions. This will provide a framework for managing the class, and the head must ensure that individuals observe this and any internal requirements. If on a visit to the school a governor saw a member of staff doing something dangerous or illegal (like smacking) there might be a case for a quiet word. But not otherwise. I don't really think this is a resignation issue and many governors will understand how the incident happened. Just apologise and regard it as part of the learning process. I doubt whether the head will think so badly of you on sober reflection. Remember she has to cope day by day with many problems, including a teacher under stress and behaving uncharacteristically. Not easy.

Getting the level right

I am making myself unpopular both with the head and some colleagues. For thirty years I have kept the books for a small company and surely my expertise ought to be a great asset, not a source of bad feeling. I am on the finance committee of course, and I surely ought to chair it, but I have been bypassed. However, that is neither here nor there. I spend hours going over the budget documents (which often don't meet my standards) and find discrepancies, payments delayed, money owed to the school not chased up, and also examples of poor estimating, e.g. on repairs or fuel bills, where over-estimating leaves less money to spend on the children. Neither the head nor the finance officer appreciates my comments and the chairman has told me to lay off. Surely we are accountable for school finances and shouldn't let errors go unnoticed?

Answer

You mean well, but you may misunderstand the role of governors, at least in the area where your experience makes you sensitive. Many governors exhaust themselves trying to check up on the work people in the school are paid to do. I say 'trying' because most of us have jobs and homes to run, and could not hope to match the vigilance day by day of people working full time on accounts, teaching fractions or trying to administer fair discipline policies. That is not the level at which we should intervene, and those of us who happen to be linguists or mathematicians, accountants or lawyers, carpenters or cooks, have to bite our tongues to avoid getting drawn into operational-level arguments. Just now and then any personal expertise we may have will be gold dust, but mostly we simply need, as a group, to grasp the strategic issues. We don't check the lifebelts, so to speak. We just make sure there is a system for checking them effectively and that we have ways of monitoring the *systems*. We don't tell teachers how to teach and whom to put in detention. We discover what factors within our control can improve the conditions in which teaching takes place. We ensure that staff have adequate development support, that outcomes are properly reported to us and that there are effective systems for the monitoring of teaching quality by senior colleagues who are trained and paid to do it. Our guidelines on behaviour policy help staff deal with disturbances day by day, leaving the interpretation to them.

The same principles apply to the budget. We are of course expected to be watchful for any impropriety in the handling of money or the keeping of accounts, but otherwise our job is to ensure that available funds are *broadly* allocated in the best possible way to support children's learning, that these broad allocations are respected – with reasonable flexibility – by the staff of the school, and that the presentation of financial matters, given that we will have to justify our decisions to parents and the LEA, is understandable, honest and transparent. But I do know how hard it is for a professional in finance to keep out of the pounds and pence, the invoices and receipts. I should add that there are some curious presentational conventions about budgets in the local authority ambit which may not match your book-keeping experience, and also timing problems with payments both ways. A late electricity bill or delay in adjusting for changes in actual numbers on roll can appear to throw out the best estimates. I am sure that your keen eye will be a great asset to your governing body and the school, not just in finance but in other matters, once you can train it to look at the bigger picture and not shadow the finance officer.

Governors get a bad OfSTED report

I am head of a large primary school in an urban area. I am one of those you seem to encounter often who can't see why we have governors at all. After training and twenty-five years experience I resent the idea that untrained people brought together almost at random should have a say in professional matters. We just had our OfSTED inspection and that is my problem. I think I do a good job – running a school these days is no joyride. Children have never been worse behaved and we get no support from parents. Numbers are falling. We haven't been put in the sin-bin yet but it was a critical report with a long list of things to improve, and – the reason for this letter – a statement that our governing body is not effective and that there must be a joint effort to increase their input into school policies and ensure that they play their part in raising standards. Is that my responsibility? Is it my job to train the governors as well as everything else, for goodness' sake? If so, I should welcome your advice. Is there any kind of governor training manual for heads?

Answer

It's not your job to train them, but it *is* your job to ensure that they perform the roles the law has laid down for them. If you believe they are incapable of contributing anything I'm afraid it is very likely that what has happened to them *is* your fault. The best bunch of governors you could find might find it difficult to cope with your lack of respect for their role, but when that respect is there I have seen more 'ordinary' governing bodies than I can count make a brilliant contribution. I put 'ordinary' in quotes because I do not really accept that anybody with the commitment to give their own time to a school is ordinary. I am sorry for these harsh words but it is the only starting place I know.

Firstly of course the LEA has an obligation to provide training, and I know what your LEA offers is of high quality. I also know that they do in-house team-building sessions on request. Ideally these include the head, because nobody working in the field would accept that such training is much use unless working together is part of the head's culture and expectation. Which means you have to want to change. You say governors shouldn't have a say in 'professional matters', but they don't. They don't manage and develop the staff, decide on the teaching methods, the detailed use of the school space or the school day, or maintain order and discipline. They do appoint senior management, decide how the budget is distributed among broad objectives, develop policies to support learning and provide its social and moral framework. They should also look after the interests of parents and community and ensure that all participants in the life of the school are treated fairly and with respect. The Education Act 2002 says 'the conduct of the school is under the general direction of the governing body' and it is also held responsible for raising standards. Can you make all that real? I can't tell you how in a few lines, but the keys are honesty and trust; a willingness to work together; appropriate expectations both ways; good teamwork; involvement of governors in school life; and good communication about education issues. Three of my books may help you.* Remember schools are not unique in being accountable to representative public bodies – think of MPs, councillors, non-executive directors, trustees, juries, magistrates.

* *Basics for School Governors*, Network Educational Press, 2000; *Heads in Partnership: working with your governors for a successful school* and *School Governors: a practical guide*, both from Pearson Education, 2001. All three give practical advice, and support it with guides to law, regulations and good practice, while the last two contain discussion papers, model working documents and illustrative materials.

Open government is the best defence against speculation and malice.

Can the LEA sack me for this?

I have had a most upsetting experience as an LEA governor of long standing. I am committed to the school and play an active part. If I speak my mind at meetings everybody understands – or so I thought – that I have only the school's interests at heart, and am 100% supportive. But it seems I have upset the new head from time to time since she took over, because I am concerned that the school no longer treats parents as thoughtfully and warmly as it used to. I have no axe to grind, but I do feel that a local councillor for the ward must represent the interests of the public, and I have never before been made to feel that looking after those interests is 'speaking out of turn'. I also commented that a newly qualified teacher needed some support in controlling a difficult junior class. To cut a long story short I have been told by the LEA that they are taking me away from this governing body to serve on another school miles away 'which needs my experience'. I have a strong feeling that this is because I am seen to be rocking the boat and that I am being moved for the sake of peace. The head is very active in her union. I am not rich and cannot afford to seek legal advice, but need to know if moving a governor is legal and my rights.

Answer

If you are right in your assumption about the reasons for your proposed move – and don't dismiss the possibility that your colleagues think another school with problems is more needy – you have to accept that a new head teacher may be a bit touchy about territory, and hasn't known you long enough to understand that you

23

mean well and are really a great supporter of the school. Unfortunately the things you have been concerned about are very close to the line between governors' role and the head's, and in particular the supervision of newly qualified teachers and their development is a management matter which we encroach on tactfully if at all. And although I do agree that communication with parents and sensitivity to their feelings are things we must always watch, we have to accept that routine communication on behalf of the school is also a territorial area and has to be tackled carefully. Is it too late to tell the head you didn't mean to be intrusive in these matters, only want to help, and have been a long-term friend of the school? But also talk to the people concerned at county hall and make sure your suspicion is justified, and see if you can negotiate your way back.

But you asked about legalities, and although an elected parent or teacher governor cannot be removed, there have been a couple of court cases – and I accept that without money or powerful friends this route may not be practical – which have established that LEA and foundation governors can be dismissed, not just moved, by those who appointed them, but only for good and legal reason. (Not toeing a 'party line' was not considered enough justification.) There is the option of appealing to the Secretary of State on the ground that an LEA has behaved unreasonably, and that costs nothing, though few appeals have been successful, because the Department have taken the view that it has to be pretty serious for one elected authority to override another.

But I must say that if you have done nothing to upset staff or colleagues other than a few possibly clumsy but well-meaning incursions into territorial waters, this is all a bit heavy. I would have thought some conciliatory words all round would be better.

Support is not a right if by that your head means unquestioning endorsement by every governor. *Individual* governors are not obliged to support everything put before them, but the *governing body* is obliged to support the decisions of its majority. Your head will have to learn to live with different opinions, and dissenters on the governing body must understand that although they are entitled to their opinions, once a decision is made they must accept majority views and do their best for the school in whatever situation it finds itself.

Betrayal by a teacher governor

Our teacher governor has never respected the privacy of our meetings and has always carried everything straight back to the staffroom. This has often annoyed us but now some very tricky issues have come up and they are damaging not just to the governing body but to the school as such. One of the matters in question concerns a recent appointment and another an exclusion case. The teacher has actually spoken indiscreetly to a number of parents whose children were victims of the incident for which another boy was excluded. Because of this the head has initiated disciplinary action. We had already had enough of the reporting of meetings so we propose to vote this teacher off the governing body. Can you tell us how to proceed? What happens if she is suspended anyway?

Answer

You suggest that there is a long history of breach of confidentiality. Remember, however, that only items classified as such by the governing body – those affecting the privacy of individuals mostly – are confidential, and otherwise members are free to report decisions, provided they do so accurately and responsibly, not revealing who said what or how people voted, or anything which reflects badly on the governing body or any of its members. But the recent actions you describe do seem outside what would be considered breach of confidentiality as a governor anyway, and if proven are serious, as the school's response indicates. But there is no means of voting an elected teacher or parent governor off the governing body. Only co-optees can be sacked by their colleagues, and even this is covered by a very rigorous procedure. The school disciplinary action is a different matter, and I think you should await the outcome. If the teacher were to be dismissed, she would of course cease to be a member. If she were suspended she would be covered by new regulations made under the 2002 Act which took effect in September 2003 and these do for the first time allow a governor who has seriously offended against the rules or the ethos of the governing body to be suspended from the governing body for one year, by a majority vote of the whole governing body. Suspension as a result of disciplinary action would be considered a justification for suspension as a governor.

Can I correct misinformation given to governors?

As a teacher governor am I entitled to speak out when governors are being told things about what goes on in the school which are not correct? I don't like to see honest people misled and frankly, governors are not always given a true picture.

Answer

A subject often raised with me in whispers. I don't need to tell you that challenging senior staff publicly – or even privately – carries risks. You have to be sure of your ground and prepared for the consequences, and I also don't need to add that the truth is rarely simple and that we all see things differently. Having taken account of all this, and if the misconceptions governors go away with are likely to change the course of events to the detriment of children, you have a duty to do *something*. If it is a major and frequent complaint it would be better if a number of you who felt the same about it could first tackle it directly with those concerned within the school. I hope your non-staff colleagues ask keen questions too.

How can we cope with having to agree to things we don't believe in?

I used to enjoy being a governor but nowadays we find ourselves going along with a lot of things just because we know there is no real alternative, not because we believe they are right. For example, we are heading for a private finance takeover of building and services. I'm not the only one who thinks this is wrong and wonders whether we can be sure decisions will be made with the children's future in mind, not profit. How can we be sure we shall get the quality of services we have always tried to provide, and what happens if there is a clash between school use of facilities and profit? Specialist status is another thing we believe will be divisive among our schools and our children, but it seems that schools which reject it will lose out. Should I resign?

Answer

I know many governors who feel as you do, and I sympathise very much on the two subjects you mention. Only you can decide whether you can live with this lack of choice. Remember, though, that being a school governor has rarely meant complete freedom to act according to your conscience, even though we all sometimes imagine it used to be easier. I can just about remember when most issues used to be decided on party political lines and there weren't enough non-political appointees to make any difference. I can also remember when all the big decisions about school spending were made at town or county hall, and the range of issues on which governors had any say at all was very small. We also now have a lot of influence, not just on spending but on other things which would have been unheard of less than a generation ago – in the fields of staffing, curriculum, discipline policies, relations with parents and community. Don't give up hope of influence even on the controversial specialist status and private finance. After all, the school decides whether or not to use the selective option even if it goes down that road, will still have some input into admission principles, and can still maximise the use of its specialist status to support the chosen specialism in neighbour schools. Channel your concern into asking sharp questions about contracts for school services and especially the two key aspects you mention. If your feelings on the very political issues you mention are still too strong you will be respected, I am sure, for resigning. Otherwise, day by day you can work to make school a friendly place, a fair place and a place which conveys good messages. Over a wide field, do believe you can still make a difference.

I seem to have strayed into professional territory

As a new governor I haven't learnt everything, but I do know that we are there to improve the school's standards, and also to be 'critical friends'. I have also done my homework by listening to what parents say and doing some thinking myself about how the school could be better organised. Towards the end of term I wrote a few notes on my findings and gave them to the head. They ranged from comments on the quality of some of the teaching, to suggestions about how the timetable could be better organised to make the most of our teachers' strengths, and there were a few less serious things, like organising the service of lunches and separating age groups at break times. To my surprise the head went berserk and said he had had a long training and thirty years' experience in education, and here was a new governor telling him how to run his school. I was a bit taken aback and also rather hurt by this as I only meant to be helpful. Should I have waited a bit longer?

Answer

I'm sure you meant well, but you have certainly made a bad start and given ammunition to thousands of heads who wish we would go away! The phrase 'critical friend' can be helpful in suggesting that when people have proved their liking for you, and their concern for your welfare, any well-intentioned critical comments from them will be graciously received, but it often worries me because it encourages governors to do just what you have done.

Firstly the critical friend is the governing body, not the individual governor. No school wants twenty critical friends all with different points of view, and besides, in law only the governing body, not the individual, has any power. Things the governing body wants to change, if any, have to emerge from discussion at meetings with a proper agenda and papers, all views heard, and with majority agreement, often quite a lengthy process. Even then the matter discussed must be one which is within the governing body's authority, but the range is very wide and I am sure you will have opportunities to bring in useful points from all the thinking you have done.

All the points you quoted from your list relate to matters which are clearly professional responsibilities, not ours. The governors' role is a strategic one, planning for the school long term through policies within which teachers and other staff do their work. These include fixing the broad distribution of the budget, choosing senior staff, setting aims and targets and monitoring the school's general progress, promoting a safe and pleasant environment and laying down behaviour guidelines. Governors do not check up on how people do their jobs, though they may create systems which ensure that all the work of the school is subject to suitable internal systems of monitoring and accountability. The use day by day of the resources of time, space, people and money available within budget headings is clearly the head's responsibility. That covers the use of space, arrangement of classes and breaks, and utilisation of staff. So are the achievement of maximum teaching quality and the maintenance of discipline within governors' guidelines.

I think it would be sensible to apologise to the head and say that these were mistakes based on inexperience. Otherwise it may rankle with him and you may feel uneasy for longer than the incident warrants. I'm sure he'll respond well.

Part Two:

Problems of Representing Others

A high proportion of governors' questions are about their representative role. In the widest sense every school governor does of course represent the whole school community – the children and their parents, the staff, the neighbourhood, and the wider public who pay for education and expect a quality service.

But in addition every group represents one section of that community. The Taylor Committee, which thirty years ago looked at the whole question of school governance nationally and shaped our present system, and on which I was privileged to serve as a parent, recommended that the governing body should be a partnership of individuals representing all the stakeholders in the school – parents, staff, LEA, community, and where appropriate the founding church or other non-government provider.

Most governors are very serious about their representative role. Naturally so, because it is a big responsibility to speak for others in matters as important as children's education. All groups have a legitimate viewpoint which must be heard. But all must learn that every group, however strong its views, is only a part of the wider school community and of the governing body, and the majority will not always agree.

Huge numbers of questions come in on these issues. One centre of controversy is whether a governor is a delegate or simply a representative of the appointing group. The difference is not always understood. A delegate is obliged to speak *and vote* in accordance with the views of the appointing group. This is the position in some kinds of committees – trade union members, for instance, will be familiar with voting according to a mandate – but *not* school governing bodies, whose members are not delegates but representatives. This means that they should listen to those they represent, transmit their views in so far as these are generally held, and report back as permitted, but NOT vote automatically in accordance with constituents' wishes. In voting they must consider the interests of the whole school as they see them, which may well be different. This is particularly hard for parent governors, under pressure not just to listen to what parents want, but to make it happen.

Parent governors have particularly acute problems. Often a great deal is expected of them, e.g. that every concern about an individual child will be aired and instantly attended to. A school which communicates well with parents and their organisations, has good arrangements for hearing individual concerns, and explains from time to time the limits of governors' responsibilities, will greatly ease this problem. Parent governors should not agree to take up individual problems because they are not proper subjects for the governing body. (The exception of course is when a parent has failed to get satisfaction from the school and the case comes to the governing body under its complaints procedure.) They must encourage parents to take individual worries to the head or responsible teacher. But widely held views should be reported and discussed.

Staff governors too are often expected to champion individuals as well as convey general dissatisfactions. In a way it's harder for them than for parents because they are fewer in number and have to convey colleagues' concerns in the presence of the head teacher, who is also their boss. Some heads – I hope a minority – find the very presence of active staff governors threatening and a few try to censor what they say, or react badly to comments they see as critical. One could almost predict that for these in time the outcome will be ineffective staff representatives, because nobody else will think it worth doing. When support staff governors were belatedly recognised as important enough to warrant their own elected governor under the 1998 Act, fresh problems emerged. One was that a few heads seemed to find their presence especially challenging and tried to circumscribe their role, keeping them out of sensitive committees and discussions and forbidding any reporting back to colleagues. Meanwhile some of the new representatives misunderstood their role and tried to bring purely workplace grievances – hours, meal breaks, supervisors – to the governing body. This was very natural, given, in some cases, the nature of the work of some constituents and their isolation. But these are problems for line management and unions, not in general governing bodies, except if a formal grievance is registered.

Most **foundation governors** represent a parent church, and it is their special concern to protect the ethos of the school as seen by its founders, almost always that of a particular faith. More widely they probably see their constituents as the members and supporters of the local church and these and other parents who have chosen the school because of its denominational teaching. This is a simpler kind of representation than many, but it does sometimes involve conflicts too, especially if the school is the only one in its area and is attended by some local children whose parents are less committed to its faith than others. I do occasionally get complaints via parent governors that the amount of religious observance in the school concerned is considered by part of the parent body to be excessive – a delicate question of representation for both parent and foundation governors.

LEA governors less commonly these days represent a particular political party and are often confused about their own accountability as LEA appointees. They represent the local education service and should be particularly watchful that their own school's policies don't harm other schools or the well-being of local schools collectively. I would think it reasonable to expect them to know the LEA's policies and be prepared to say what they are, but once more they are not delegates and should put the interests of their own school first. It has certainly been made clear that they do not have to vote according to any 'party line'.

Community governors often wonder whom they represent, as they are co-opted by governing bodies with varying motives, not the least being to import knowledge – of local affairs, finance, business, etc. I would say that their main concern should be the school's impact on members of the wider public – their safety, peace, space, amenities; the effect of school plans on land use; its pupils' behaviour outside school; its relationship with householders, the elderly, local shops. But once more, all points of view should be heard, and if there is conflict the school's interest comes first.

Confidentiality often comes up, and many governors ask whether, when and how they can report what goes on at meetings. Heads sometimes overdo the confidentiality issue. It needs to be better understood that most governors' business is not confidential at all, but that items classified as such (mostly involving individual privacy) should be protected at all costs. Other decisions are not confidential and minutes become public property once the chair has approved them, but reports should still never put the governing body or any member in a bad light or highlight dissension. In short, secrecy only exceptionally, but corporate loyalty always. Staff members in particular should resist the temptation to entertain colleagues with highly coloured accounts of who out-smarted the head, who lost her temper, or who made a fool of himself at the meeting. Once again, school management could reduce problems by being more proactive themselves, giving parents and other interested parties prompt information about important, non-confidential matters. Open government is the best defence against speculation and malice.

Our staff governors aren't allowed to speak

My head teacher knows I am writing to you and I have already told him frankly about my concerns. We have two governors representing teaching staff and one the support staff. I know them well (as a long-serving chair who is very involved in the school outside meetings) and they are eminently sensible people. I'm sure they could make a valuable contribution, and before I knew the head had a problem with it I often used to make a point of asking them how the staff felt about this or that. They always replied non-committally but I now understand that the head has told them they are not allowed to speak at governors' meetings off their own bat, that he speaks for 'the school', and that he is prepared to vet any statement they wish to make beforehand. Am I right to be concerned about this? We will both accept what you say.

Answer

Yes, you are right to be concerned. I know there are many heads who feel
threatened by uncensored debate, and with all the responsibilities they bear I can
just about understand it, especially if they have ever had a disillusioning
experience. I am only surprised that after about twenty years of statutory staff
governors some still haven't learnt to live with it. I can only assure you that every
individual appointed to a school governing body is there in his or her own equal
and independent right, and that staff governors should not be treated differently
from parents, church foundation governors, LEA or co-opted governors, who are
all expected to contribute freely from their distinctive viewpoint.

What can I say to help your head accept this? Firstly that I think that it is healthier
in the end if staff have a forum in which they can speak for colleagues on matters
concerning the school – not purely individual workplace grievances, as I often say,
since there are other routes to solving these – and that in my experience it breeds
loyalty rather than the reverse. Muttering can be much more subversive, or even
worse, approaching individual governors, which frustrated staff often quite
wrongly do. It's also my experience that you get much better quality staff
governors in a school where the head welcomes their contribution and there is
also no suspicion of a price to pay if you speak out of turn. The message soon
gets round that it's a meaningless chore and the result is that you get people who
have nothing much to say anyway. I have known schools go through cycles of
effective and ineffective staff governors as heads change, and an outsider can spot
the reason at once.

Secondly I think you might repeat – and share with your staff governors – that I
would always advise any governor, and particularly a staff governor, to warn the
head in advance if they feel bound to make an unexpected controversial statement
about any major issue, or even repeat a critical comment they have heard outside.
I think this is an act of courtesy which does no harm and may reassure those who
find uncensored discussion a bit threatening. But it still must not be censorship!

> The best recruiting agency is the reputation of the current governing
> body, so everything you do as head to influence its self-image, its style, the
> quality of its work and – vitally – its visibility in the school, will alter the
> way people perceive it. If the governing body is a pretence it will attract
> pretenders, if it's a battlefield it will tempt aggressors, if it is a shambles it
> will recruit muddlers, and if it is treated with respect it will attract people
> worthy of respect.

Do LEA governors have to toe a party line?

I realise that not all LEA governors come from party networks but in our area most do. The ones on our governing body can be helpful when the matters discussed don't impinge on LEA policy, but they are not willing to take part when that policy is under discussion (much less support us in occasionally seeking changes). Indeed they often say they must keep out of such discussions because of conflict of interest. As head teacher I find this frustrating, and I would like to know whether they are correct in implying that – unlike other governors in my experience – they are not governors in the full sense of the word. I find it hurtful, as for the rest of us the school comes first.

Answer

A very interesting question. When I was asked by a county LEA some time ago to write a booklet specially for their LEA governors I couldn't find guidance anywhere, so was left to my own thoughts and reasonings.

Which were as follows. No governor is a delegate. Many governors besides LEA ones – parents and teachers especially – have a representative role, which means they have to do their best to understand and pass on the views of those who put them there, but in deciding how to act they must be guided only by the needs of the school *as they see them*, i.e. support when they honestly can, feel free to dissent if they must. So I sympathise totally with the frustrations you express, and I agree that LEA representatives sometimes seem to be escaping responsibility by citing conflict of interest. An LEA representative, whether or not a political nominee, should in my view do his or her best to know and understand the LEA's policies on any matters affecting schools, and be equipped to interpret them to colleagues. When that representative is actually a councillor there may also be rare occasions when a very delicate or confidential issue of party policy comes up and the member is not free to take part at all. We must accept that. But when an established policy of the LEA harms the school's interest, I personally would like to see that colleague, if he or she shares our concern, do everything possible to help us. I have been lucky enough at several critical times to work with party nominees of all parties who have been very courageous in following their consciences on issues affecting the school. Many years ago my very first chair was actually so concerned about the effect proposed cuts would have on our school that he spoke against them within his party, though a prominent member.

I am supported in this interpretation by two legal cases involving attempts by a church foundation in one case and an LEA in the other to remove governors they had nominated. In one case it was for not voting according to the policies of the appointing body on important school issues. In the other it was a straight replacement of a party nominee when control of the council changed. The judgements included some useful legal opinions, namely that an appointed governor could be removed if s/he had ceased to be generally representative of the appointing body (e.g. because the council had changed hands), but that such a governor could *not* be removed for having taken an independent line in the discussion and decisions of the governing body. As far as I know these judgements have never been overtaken, and I hope they will not be. Most of us welcome the fact that LEAs now appoint far more of their governors from outside the party networks, but it is good to know that the local councillor governor, if we are lucky enough to have one, need not fear undue pressure to conform in matters of conscience.

> You get much better quality staff governors in a school where the head welcomes their contribution and there is no suspicion of a price to pay if you speak out of turn.

I've upset everybody

As a parent governor I take very seriously my duty to keep parents informed, and also the need to observe total silence on items classified as confidential. At our last meeting we had an item about the possibility that our primary school might have to expand to three form entry: a large area of nearby land is earmarked for housing, and starter and 3-bedroom homes are already going up like mushrooms. (It was not classified and nobody mentioned secrecy.) Everybody can see what is happening and parents are bound to ask questions, and indeed they did at the PTA meeting I routinely attended a week later. In answer to questions I said that we had been discussing the implications for the school, and expansion to 3 fe had been mooted, but that no decisions had been made. The head and the chair are furious with me, say it was totally irresponsible to stir up concern in that way, and that controversial issues should remain secret until there was something definite to report. Was I wrong?

Answer

I can understand how upset you are. You are right in saying that if a document doesn't say it's confidential, it isn't. What's more, the agenda and the papers which go with it are public documents and must be available to *anybody* who asks, not just parents, with only classified material omitted, and so must the minutes once the chair has approved them. 'Confidential' is intended mostly for private matters concerning individuals, and in general not (save in exceptional cases, e.g. contracts still being negotiated) things which some might find inconvenient to have discussed before they are ready. So I can assure you that you haven't done anything wrong, and I know it's very upsetting to be told you must deceive your fellow parents.

After saying all that, life isn't always so simple. Governors who may not have been present feel upstaged if they aren't the first to know, and you have to live with them. Chair and head are human and don't want the pot boiling over before they've had time to adjust the switches. So I'd always try to talk to a few people beforehand, particularly the head and chair, about the imminent PTA meeting, the fact that when houses are springing up under your noses there's bound to be speculation, which is usually more damaging than the truth, and the folly and dubious legality of keeping public documents away from those who have most right to know. I'd also keep very close to my fellow parent governors and try to adopt a common policy – at least then they can't pretend to be somewhere else when you want some support. But if possible I'd try to go back further still – only of course when the 'secret' is a community matter and not an individual's privacy – and urge upon all concerned the good sense of keeping parents in the picture as soon as there's any cause for speculation. Rumour and mistrust are so much more damaging, and secrecy creates still more problems. If you don't classify the papers, how do you record the discussion in the minutes? Often, I've found, in a way that nobody outside could understand. That increases the mistrust and you get the worst of both worlds.

I know the doghouse isn't the best place to spend the night. But you can say you are sorry you upset people, as long as you don't accept that what you did was against the rules. Above all use the opportunity to stimulate some clear thinking about these community issues, and how counterproductive such half-measures of secrecy are. At the very least you can agree a clearly understood policy acceptable to all members.

> Staff members in particular should resist the temptation to entertain colleagues with highly coloured accounts of who outsmarted the head at the meeting, who lost her temper, or who made a fool of himself.

A parent governor's familiar questions

I am a new parent governor and I seem to be in trouble already. Ours is the first stage of a brand new school. My two fellow PGs are men and work in the town so I get all the mums' concerns. I am now getting approached by quite a number, and, anxious to do a good job, I try to represent them as best I can. Sometimes I have to be a bit aggressive to find a place in the meeting where I can air some parent worries, all very natural ones in the circumstances. Things like whether there is a qualified first-aider available (it is a primary school); adequate midday supervision, open gates, dogs on site (there are builders still about); when there are going to be hot lunches; how the children are arranged in tables (seems to be some kind of 'streaming'); and also lots of worries about individual children who may be timid, frightened of bullying, have some health or language problem or exceptional ability (of course). Whatever my opinion, I think it is my job to help. But I have had some very clear vibes from the head and other governors that this is not the right place or time and that somehow I have got it wrong. Please help me.

Answer

Oh dear! These are such familiar problems with new parent governors, especially those who are caring and conscientious – and brave as well. First, please don't feel you have done anything which can't be put right. There are two issues here, one to do with queries (first aid, lunches, safety) which are general, legitimate and natural in the unusual circumstances, and these are definitely things which you have to find some way of airing. The others, the child with health problems or fears or exceptional ability, are the bread and butter of any parent governor's life but you must not try to bring them up at governors' meetings. Hard though it is, you must say to parents, 'I'm sorry, but the governors deal with school policies affecting all children, and if you have a concern about your own child you must take it up yourself with the head or class teacher. If it can't be solved to your satisfaction you may then complain formally to the governors, but there is no slot in the meeting for individual concerns.' Otherwise you will have no peace and you will be always in the doghouse with your governor colleagues for bringing up inappropriate things outside the agenda. Even legitimate governor business about safety, provision of lunches, first aid, etc. must be programmed as an agenda item – do not be afraid to ask for this.

But your letter concerns me in that it does suggest that parents of this brand new school have not been very well served on the information front. In the circumstances their concerns are natural and correct. I am surprised that they are not brought together from time to time for information, reassurance and answers to general queries, that there is no time set aside when individual queries can be brought in, and that there is not a regular newsletter. Perhaps you and your fellow parent governors could tactfully suggest these to the head (always act together where you can). In any case you could ask for a short item on every agenda on progress in settling in, which would give you material to answer questions and an opportunity to ask your own. These days parents rightly expect to be kept in the picture, and not just on practical things like safety and lunch arrangements but also on teaching methods and organisation. Can you find a likely parent or group to start an association?

> Expectations are the key to defining, maintaining and enriching a relationship.

Problems of a church school governor

I am a parent member of the foundation group in an aided school in town and another aided school in a village. I am active in the church and thought I understood my role, but I am now very confused about the system and where my loyalty lies. The town school has immensely high standards reflected in SATs scores, so is oversubscribed, the village one is smaller but able to take all comers. You can imagine the Sunday church congregation in the town is growing! I helped draw up the allocation criteria and I think they were fair. Among those with a genuine history of church attendance we took those living nearest. Now people blame me for not looking after parent interests. In the other school at least half just see it as a village school and have no church connection, and some resent the time spent on religious education and worship and also fund-raising for everlasting roof repairs. Again I get blamed.

Answer

I would say these are becoming fairly common problems in church schools and may well increase. Some, like your town one, are under pressure because of ever-increasing parental interest in school performance and anxieties about behaviour. Positive choosers may well improve further the performance of already good church schools. (I assume yours can't easily expand?) On the other hand the one-school village will often experience a decline, proportionately, in real believers, if they become commuter or second-home territory through fashion or re-siting of companies, so that both religious observance and fund-raising become more controversial.

As a foundation governor who is also a parent you have a difficult role. In both schools the main need must be for parents to understand what the system is and why – in general they don't – and perhaps a meeting of interested parents at the beginning of the allocation process would help. Maybe this is something to discuss with the diocesan schools officer. One point to make is that the church provided these schools initially and in consideration of this has always been allowed to give preference to families of its own faith as well as teach it. (In many countries publicly provided schools don't teach religion at all and church schools are fee-paying, while parents here have a choice within the state system.) If a popular church school were to expand, church members would have to find some of the funds, and they also have to help pay for repairs. As for the village, it is inevitable that where a wide range of people use the local school, some are less keen on the religious observances than others, but *all* schools by law have to offer worship and religious education, and parents do have a right to opt out of these. What's more, all schools fund-raise, but it isn't compulsory to participate. One could have a debate on the rights and wrongs of all this, but it's the system we have and it helps a great deal if people understand it.

It sounds as if your town allocation is as fair as you can devise in the circumstances and although there is of course provision for parents to appeal and/or to challenge the criteria I wouldn't hold out a great deal of hope in the circumstances. I won't say 'try to interest some of the disappointed town parents in the village' (a) because it probably isn't practical and (b) if it were it might create another problem of insufficient places for village children. I understand your dilemma as a parent member of the foundation group. Establishing and considerably increasing these was an attempt to bring parental influence in aided schools nearer to the level of community schools, but of course it isn't the same as an elected parent governor with no dual loyalty. In the end you are there to see that the aims of the school's founders are observed, but you also have to spread awareness of parents' feelings among your fellow foundation members, and also keep in close touch with your elected parent governors.

Some heads – I hope a minority – find the very presence of active staff governors threatening and a few try to censor what they say or react badly to comments they see as critical. One could almost predict that for these in time the outcome will be ineffective staff representatives, because nobody else will think it worth doing.

Role of a community governor

I am a co-opted governor – now, I believe, called a community governor. I think I am the only genuine article – I don't mean anything critical by that but the other co-optees in my time have been valued ex-parents no longer eligible for election, ex-LEA governors whose party lost the council, or experts of various kinds, all very good I must add. I have served a long time but always been a bit uncertain of my role, and now I urgently need clarification. The school is bursting at the seams and the LEA is planning to build new accommodation on adjoining land. This will definitely be detrimental to the amenities of the whole community, which is not blessed with much open space, and this land, which the council own, was originally designated, a small amount for a day centre for the elderly to replace unsuitable old accommodation, and the rest to remain public open space. Children and young people, dog-walkers, anybody after a bit of fresh air, will suffer, not to mention the old people. This doesn't seem to worry my fellow 'community' governors, who think the school's desperate shortage of accommodation is overriding. Should I be supporting the objectors? Do I really represent the 'community', whatever that may mean?

Answer

I suspect that most schools are ready in suitable cases to co-opt ex-parents with a proven record of commitment to the school, ex-LEA nominees whose party is no longer in power (though I would hope, indeed I am sure, that party political appointments as such are increasingly uncommon), and people with expertise which the school would welcome access to. Some are even glad to have offers from volunteers with none of this background who have expressed an interest and a desire to be involved in a school. There's nothing wrong with any of this. (I know you don't think there is either.) I have always thought of co-opted governors as representing the wider community and my LEA indeed has always used the term, which the law has now adopted. I would expect them not only to bring experience gained outside education, but also to show knowledge of and consideration for the school's neighbours in the widest sense. In particular they can ensure that the governing body doesn't forget the impact the school has on the community and its scope for avoiding annoyance to neighbours, involving local people in its big events, and supporting local causes. There will also be times when community governors can draw the school's attention to conflicts of interest, as now in your school.

Having said all that, I have to emphasise that no member of the governing body is a delegate with an obligation to vote for a sectional interest, not even elected teachers and parents. All governors bring a particular experience to the common task, all must listen to the views of those they represent and make them known if they are strong and widely held, but in the end the guiding light for every governor when judging options is the well-being of their school as they see it. I don't think it's any different for you, though your 'constituency' is more amorphous than that of other groups. It is legitimate, indeed right, for you always to consider the effect of the school's plans on other interests and to report the expressed views of other groups in the community, but in the end you consider the school's needs and the best way of meeting them. Those groups will of course have an opportunity for formal objection to the plan.

A staff governor and staff grievances

I have been staff governor for 18 months. I am a special educational needs assistant and confess I did not realise at first that I would be representing staff like cleaners and site workers. However, I have tried hard to 'put myself about' and inform everybody about the agenda in advance. For instance, when we considered changes in the school day I consulted widely and reported all the comments, which as you can imagine came from many conflicting points of view. As an ex-teacher I was sad that they were all about personal convenience rather than the children's education. Now I find I am getting into deep water. Currently I have an item from our assistant schoolkeeper which is really a complaint about how he is treated by his boss and various things about his duties; one from a technician saying that he has a load of menial jobs quite unlike what he thought the post involved; and one from the canteen manager about the pupils' rude and dangerous behaviour in the dining room. Am I supposed to get these items on the agenda, take them up privately or forget them?

Answer

I sympathise very much. Many of the new staff governors – who really need some training of their own – feel the same. You seem to have been very conscientious, and the problem which now worries you is universal – how to deal with largely workplace issues coming from varied small groups with real but very limited viewpoints. I think you strike the right note when you imply that in your eyes the governing body's job is advancing the children's education. On the other hand a big school by its nature employs people who are remote from this, though they are all essential parts of the team and need to feel that they are listened to and cared for. Somehow you have to find a balance. It was quite right to consult carefully about the school day, but I would consider that two of the three other items you quote are not matters initially for the governing body but the sort of workplace niggles which inevitably arise. It is not a works committee. Nevertheless, many staff may well in innocence think you are there to solve these problems, one way or another.

The assistant schoolkeeper and technician issues are for line management to sort out initially – and there will be either a member of senior management staff or a bursar/general manager ultimately in charge of these activities if representations lower down the line fail. You can perhaps smooth the path here, just as parent governors sometimes do outside the governing body with parents who need to bring purely individual concerns to the head. If this approach also fails, a reference to their union or a formal grievance procedure may be necessary. The canteen manager's case is a little different, because apart from safety the pupils' behaviour in any part of the premises *is* an educational issue. I think you should raise this first with the head, and it may be that if the governing body has a pastoral or student affairs committee it should be discussed there. It might be a good idea – certainly when the next election of a staff governor comes up – for the head to speak to the support staff as a group about the role of their representative and dispel some natural misunderstandings. Otherwise the person elected will be under a lot of pressure, or the governing body will be overloaded with inappropriate grumbles which are almost endemic among the small groups of people who work remotely from the main activity in any institution.

Governing bodies don't manage and develop the staff, decide on the teaching methods, the detailed use of the school space or the school day, or maintain order and discipline. They do appoint senior management, decide how the budget is distributed among broad objectives, develop policies to support learning and provide its social and moral framework. They should also look after the interests of parents and community and ensure that all participants in the life of the school are treated fairly and with respect. The Education Act 2002 says 'the conduct of the school is under the general direction of the governing body' and it is also held responsible for raising standards.

Parent governors in the firing line

I expect my query is an old one, but I'm a new parent governor! Already it seems to me that parent governors get all kicks and no ha'pence. We are kept out of sensitive activities on the ground that our child is in that class, or we live in that street or something else that sounds equally like an excuse. We get a lot of criticism for taking up time with parents' complaints, for bringing our own children into everything, for not being interested in long-term issues, and are generally made to feel like a nuisance. What are our rights and what makes a good parent governor? Am I unreasonable to expect my share of the action and a bit of appreciation?

Answer

I don't know about appreciation – governors rarely get much of that. But you are certainly entitled to expect your share of the action. All governors – apart from a few restrictions on people who work in the school – are equal in their right to contribute – and the kind of reasons given for excluding you from particular tasks seem to me to be feeble in the extreme. I do believe that in many schools parent governors get the worst of any stick that's going. Indeed, some heads responding to a survey picked them out as being especially problematic. It's only fair to say that at a personal level I've also been told by many heads that parents are the heart of their governing bodies, caring more, doing the lion's share of the work, being good ambassadors. But I'm talking now about heads who are governor-friendly. Those who are not may find it easy to vent their frustration on an object so near home, and especially inconvenient to deal with people who know the school so well.

I'd be the first to agree that many new parent governors make innocent but tiresome mistakes. Some may think they can achieve things on their own (and other parents may expect it), not realising that nothing can be changed except by the governing body acting as one. Others may not understand that governors can only be effective at a strategic level and are not there to check up on what goes on in the classroom, the playground or the office. Many may see the governing body as a sort of complaints committee and waste its time with streams of individual concerns which ought to go directly to the head or teacher. Most start by seeing the school through the eyes of their children – but I always say we waited a long time for that kind of passion and direct experience – and find it hard to get the big picture in focus. A few have the bad habit of springing things on the head without warning at a meeting.

Remember these things, but don't compromise on your right to listen to parents' *general* concerns and raise them when relevant agenda items are being discussed. If necessary, propose such items. Don't shrink from home truths when they are necessary to the matter being discussed. Ensure that you do get your 'share of the action' – ask your fellow governors to support you by rejecting trivial reasons for excluding you. After all, school communities are small and most governors from time to time have to deal with things that come close to home. You only need withdraw from a task or discussion if there is some reason special to you which would cast doubts on your impartiality. In short, you are a full and equal governor with the added responsibility of representing some very important people in the school community. But do watch the beginners' mistakes.

A parent governor's place on the agenda

As a parent governor I think I was elected to look after parents' interests, and I was therefore pleased to find that in this school the regular agenda had an item 'Parent Governors' Report'. My fellow parent governors were quite willing to let me deal with this item and they sometimes let me have their contributions. I also collect quite a large number of my own at the gate and round about, and I did say in my little election CV that I was determined to get parents' comments heard. These may be general complaints about school policies but more often they are about the treatment of individual children. However, the head does not like my reports and said I was not a one-woman complaints committee. She said the item was intended to be a very short statement about general matters like the amount raised at the fete or drawing attention to the good work done on decorating and the like in Saturday morning working parties. Is she within her rights? I think she only wants compliments.

Answer

The head is correct in saying that the governing body is not the place to air a miscellany of individual parents' critical comments for the first time. Whether it is her job to correct you is another matter. It isn't really the head's job to tell governors how their meeting is handled. It would have been better coming from the chair. Leaving that aside, I really think that you have misunderstood the purpose of your slot. You have a very important role as a sounding-board for *general* parent concerns and are fortunate to have a place in the agenda for these, as well as PTA activity such as the head suggested. Where appropriate you can report the reactions of parents as a whole in so far as you know them to any important changes in school practice or rules, e.g. modifications to uniform, a new school meals contract, a new reading scheme, though these would only come up occasionally.

But it certainly is wrong for parent governors to see themselves as carriers of individual complaints, which initially should not be channelled through governors at all. A good school will encourage parents to come in personally, and a good governing body will have had a complaints policy for a long time – it has become compulsory at last. But that will only cover matters which have already been brought to the head or another member of staff and failed to have a satisfactory outcome.

Obviously parents *will* approach their elected governors with all sorts of concerns, and occasionally there will be a *widespread* outcry about some new practice which a conscientious governor must bring up, but even this should not be sprung

44

on the head without prior warning at a governors' meeting. That is inconsiderate and unlikely to get a good response. Warn her first, and ask for it to be on the agenda if it can't readily be solved. Parents should be encouraged to go to the appropriate teacher or the head in the first instance, unless of course the governor can answer the query from personal knowledge on the spot. In an extreme case of timidity you might perhaps offer to go with them, but in this case do make it clear that it is only for company and not to support the complaint.

> Support is not a right if by that your head means unquestioning endorsement by every governor. *Individual* governors are not obliged to support everything put before them, but the *governing body* is obliged to support the decisions of its majority. Your head will have to learn to live with different opinions, and dissenters on the governing body must understand that although they are entitled to their opinions, once a decision is made they must accept majority views and do their best for the school in whatever situation it finds itself.

Problems of teacher governors

I wonder whether most teacher governors have the problems we have locally. What they amount to essentially is a desire by colleagues (and particularly the head) to restrict teacher representatives; to keep them off certain committees; to deny their right to bring staff concerns to the governing body; and censor their contributions, either by insisting they clear them in advance or carpeting them for speaking 'out of turn'. When you came to speak to teacher governors in our LEA you gave us a lot of encouragement, and as a result many of us are now clearer about our status and have more confidence to claim equality, but the pressures don't get any less.

Answer

I remember the sessions in your LEA and how shocked I was at first about the things some of you had been told. I agree that pressures on staff governors have not diminished. One reason may be the election, a few years ago, of the first support staff representatives in every school – which of course was long overdue. This may have sharpened the anxiety of more timid heads (and some more traditional governors) about discussing school affairs in a wider forum. It upsets me to think that school class distinctions remain so sharp that a few find it even more threatening to have to share delicate matters with midday supervisors and grounds staff, say (though remember the new governors are also technicians, bursars and business managers!), than teacher colleagues. That may be why we still, after all these years, hear of attempts to keep staff governors out of committees, confidential items, and so on, as well as trying to censor what they say and report. Remember that at the same time schools had to accommodate all the new delicacies of performance management and pay decisions, so those who had these fears felt them even more acutely. I hate saying all this. It isn't nice. But if you doubt its truth, ask yourself where the pressures have come from to limit support staff representation, remove teachers' right to be elected parent governors, and diminish all governors' role in appointments and staff discipline.

At least the law and regulations treat all governors equally. The minor exceptions – even these in my view unnecessary – are the exclusion of employees from chairing committees and from the pay and appraisal of individual colleagues (but *not* from membership of the relevant committees). Like other governors, they do not have to treat everything as secret, only items classified as confidential, but of course any reporting must be loyal and responsible. Like other governors, they have to keep out of any discussions from which they might stand to gain personally and from matters where circumstances would make it difficult for them to be impartial. As representatives they may bring staff views on agenda items to the governing body, but they are not delegates and are free to express their own honest opinions and vote in what they personally see as the best interests of the school. Those heads who find it easy and natural to accept these principles – and there are many – have as their reward the uniquely valuable contribution staff governors make to discussion. They can also spread sound information about the reasons behind decisions among their colleagues and thus prevent the misunderstanding and ill-founded resentment which secrecy brings with it.

When you've been round the track a few times you realise that without a maintenance plan a governing body is like an old house: something is always leaking, creaking or falling apart.

Can they exclude teacher governors when an item is confidential?

I am quite an experienced teacher governor, but something happened the other day which has never occurred before. Towards the end of the meeting (of the full governing body) we came to an item about 'the future of the school' and the chairman, who is new, said it should be treated as confidential. Then to my astonishment he said the observers and the teacher governor would in that case have to leave. I was stunned, too stunned I suppose to ask why, and we meekly left the room.

46

There was another teacher who had been asked to come for an item on her subject and the chairman of the PTA who left with me, but the deputy, who is there as an observer, didn't move. Nobody challenged it. Our borough is short of primary school places, and if a new school were built or others expanded, it could mean closure for our school, which is the wrong side of town for the growing population, with a railway and level crossing between. Maybe they thought it might be bad for teacher morale if these possibilities were openly discussed, but rumour is rife.

Answer

The worst thing for teacher morale is rumour and uncertainty and lack of proper communication. But the simple answer to your question is that no governor should be excluded from a confidential item except (a) on a matter in which an appeal might ensue (e.g. grievance, discipline, exclusion), making it necessary to keep enough governors 'clean' to hear the appeal – and normally for this reason these would be discussed in a committee, not full governors – or (b) where the governor might gain personally from the outcome.

So your chair was in error and in any case he should not have presumed to make that decision himself – it is for all the governors. Incidentally that shows how important it is that *all* governors know the rules thoroughly: an ill-informed or even ill-motivated chair can otherwise rob them of their right to participate. It was a particularly bad error, since it created first- and second-class governors and implied that certain governors were less trustworthy than others. Visitors should be asked to leave for confidential items, and your deputy should have left with the other non-governors. Again you see how a procedural mistake can lead to something more fundamental going wrong, in this case altering the balance of interest through the presence of a non-governor member of staff.

What can you do? You can show my reply to your chair if you feel brave enough. If, as I suspect, you would find that hard I think you could usefully discuss it with your head, who would be able to mount a challenge with more authority next time than you could alone. You could also tell some of your fellow governors, and add how important it is with a new chair for others to be sure of their ground. I am sure you will cope next time.

Must a teacher governor always follow the staff line?

As a teacher governor I am conscientious about consulting in the staff-room about matters coming up before governors and never fail to pass on staff views. So far I have always been in agreement with colleagues, but now we are considering a plan to shorten the lunch break, unusually long in our school. We are not curtailing the school day or increasing taught time, but using extra time after lessons for sport and clubs, and also making staff available, when not committed to such activities, for support with homework, revision guidance, library, etc. Over-long lunch breaks often give rise to behaviour problems when few staff are on duty, and parents have strongly supported the new plan. I must add that our school day will still be no longer and our lunch-hour no shorter than the city norm. Most of the staff are against it but I really believe that it will improve the quality of life for our children in a deprived inner city, so I want to speak up for it. But is this fair to those I represent?

Answer

Yes, it is, as long as you faithfully report what the rest of the staff think and ensure that this is recorded. In the end, once parent and teacher governors have reported the views of their groups, they should act according to conscience and the interests of the school as a whole. I always admire teacher governors who have the detachment to look at issues independently once in a while and the courage to follow them through – and of course sometimes risk not being re-elected. After all, in the end we are there for the children. I have found that teachers' attitudes do change when they see a real improvement in the quality of children's school lives, even if the means has not been welcome. Do what you believe right but do not judge your colleagues prematurely or too harshly. I am sure many already use the time at midday for clubs, lesson preparation or marking.

Parent governors get the blame

I think there is a current of feeling against governors. I want to make a point particularly about parent governors. Some years ago I saw a heads' survey in which they said in effect that it's parent governors who cause most trouble, that we are only there to advance our own children, that we pass on school-gate gossip, etc. etc. Our head is as bad as the rest, yet we parent governors do the annual report to parents with almost no interest from the others, we do all the exclusion hearings, go to all the big events, and play a full part while others just nod and mutter. And I don't know anybody who became a parent governor to get favours for their own children. Do we have to put up with this?

Answer

You may exaggerate the scale of this, but I do know it goes on. In fairness, some heads tell me everywhere I go that their parents are the ones who keep the show going, do most of the work, understand the issues, etc. But I also hear all about parent governors seeing things in terms of their own children, having short-term goals, interfering in day-by-day management, and being indiscreet. Why? I think a lot of heads who'd like governors to go away altogether vent their frustration on parents, who are handy targets, captive audience, not able to take offence and go. There's also the point that those who directly represent others are seen as more threatening. Parent governors may also care more, know the school better and be less easy to discourage or fob off by the small number of heads who have that in mind. If you are unlucky enough to meet one of these, just point out, as you have to me, the contribution you make and how unfair they are.

I also think we all need to work hard to see that the comments are never deserved. That means making sure we don't make the kind of mistakes we are accused of and being brave enough to counsel (perhaps new) colleagues who do. I do think there is a tendency to see the school from one's own children's standpoint and sometimes to be too short term. I tell heads that we waited a long time for that passion and first-hand knowledge to be on governing bodies, and there's a place for it. But we must keep the big picture in focus. Also, parent representatives sometimes don't know how to handle concerns parents bring to them. If they are general points involving school policy or practice, discussion should be programmed through the agenda. If they are not policy matters they shouldn't come to the governing body at all except as the final stage of a formal complaint. Purely individual concerns should be taken up with the head directly by the parents concerned; a governor can reassure or go with them if they are timid. No governor should ever spring anything on the head without warning at a meeting – that's very bad – or try to get it in as AOB unless it's only just come up and delay would be really serious.

All of us must also be careful not to try to solve things ourselves outside the governing body and remember that as individuals we have no power. We must make sure we keep to strategic issues and not stray into day-by-day management. Finally, we must never reveal any personal matters which come to our ears. We are privileged in our access to the school and, like teachers, must be discreet.

> Most cases of provocative intrusion arise not from *governing body* error but from enthusiastic beginners who believe that they can somehow or other put things right on their own.

Some more equal than others

You've answered many questions about the new staff governors, but as one fairly recently elected (because the first felt an outsider and resigned after two meetings!) I want to tell you that there are still a lot of problems and we desperately need support and clarification of our role. Are we really full and equal governors? I've been told I cannot be on the staffing committee legally, for a start. I could understand if a member of staff were involved in a grievance or discipline case, but the staffing committee deals with all sorts of general things, how staff are deployed, appointments arrangements, creating new jobs or combining jobs, sickness and maternity, supply, all very central to school affairs. In my innocence I thought staff governors who know the school would be especially useful in these discussions. I'm told I can't be on an appointments panel or clerk a committee which, being quite senior in the school office, I could do well enough. I've also been told it isn't 'appropriate' for me to be on curriculum because I'm not a teacher, or on finance because I work alongside the finance officer. The chair and head between them are responsible for all this: other governors would back me if sure of their ground.

The previous appointee resigned for these reasons but also because he wasn't allowed to bring up any matters of concern to other groups he represented and was excluded from confidential items.

Answer

This makes me angry. Some LEAs do run training courses specially for the new staff governors and I now wish more did: I have taken part in some and I'm sorry to say I have heard of all these appalling goings-on. I can only assure you again that you are in every sense a full and equal governor. There is no excuse for excluding you for confidential items or from any general school committees or from discussion of any item other than one from which you might personally stand to gain or be too close to be impartial. This last applies to us all. *There are in fact no restrictions which apply to staff governors as such.* There are restrictions, just a few, which apply to anyone employed in the school (including the head and teachers). These are that they can't be chair, they can't clerk the governing body, they can't become co-opted governors and they can't be present for the discussion of an *individual's* pay or appraisal (though they can be on the relevant committees). They can clerk committees. Otherwise, like all other governors, they have to absent themselves if they stand to gain personally from a decision or have a direct conflict of interest.

I would just like to add one thing about your colleague who resigned. He may have tried to bring up a lot of support staff concerns about their own work, conditions or treatment which aren't really governor business, i.e. more appropriate to line management, employer, a trade union or a grievance committee. Or he may in honesty have wanted to put the record straight on some matter where he thought the governors hadn't been told the whole truth. Both natural. But the governing body has a role only in policy matters which directly or indirectly concern the children's education. I have picked up this common misconception from staff governor training.

> All governors bring a particular experience to the common task, all must listen to the views of those they represent and make them known if they are strong and widely held, but in the end the guiding light for every governor when judging options is the well-being of their school as they see it.

A parent governor's dilemma

Ours is a popular infants school in a prosperous area where many parents are high up in their professions and ambitious for their children. They put quite a lot of pressure on the head and staff, and I'm bound to say the governors, about anything they don't like. Many take their children into the private sector at seven, though they are very happy to use the local infants school, which is excellent. I try to be tactful but I sometimes feel very unhappy about taking up issues which seem to be based on parents' ambitions for particular children rather than the good of all. Then I remember that these parents gave me their votes and expect me to deliver. This has now been made very clear over a hot issue. We have two parallel Reception classes and of course there is a fairly wide age range depending on birthdays. Our fairly new head is keen to keep each class a random age mix, rather than having one taking the slightly older beginners, and a few of the families I've mentioned have taken it into their heads that their children are among the more advanced and also, as it happens, among the older ones. They would like the latter segregated so that they can advance faster. The children concerned have been two to three years in private nurseries. The parents have asked me to support them. Should I take this up? After all, they voted for me.

51

Answer

Parent governors are representatives, not delegates. You must listen to what all parents say, but when it comes to which points of view to support, try to judge what is in the best interests of *all* the children. I won't comment on the pros and cons of this issue, though I'm sure your head, in preferring a mix, is working on the basis that children vary enormously in maturity between four and five anyway, with early experiences playing a major part. Mixing them may be fairer and indeed may work better. But even if it were more than a minority point of view – in which case you might give it an airing – you have to remember that the arrangement of classes and the grouping of children generally is a professional matter which we should leave to head and staff.

The kind of neighbourhood you describe is one where you will be under a lot of pressure from groups with a particular preoccupation, and as time goes on, if you are not careful, you will also be inundated with requests to take up issues on behalf of individual children. You must be firm. The governing body deals with policy issues affecting all children, and governors who forget this are likely to lose what influence they have, to the detriment of all. Individual problems and complaints must be firmly re-directed towards the class teacher or head, and when a relevant issue comes before governors all must vote for the best option as they see it for all the children.

It might be worth discussing with your head how to get this message across to parents generally. If she were to talk to them when elections are imminent about what is and isn't reasonable to expect of governors, it would be a great help. It would be better still if the school also set up an hour a week when there would always be a staff member available to deal with individual questions and worries, both taking the pressure off governors and reminding people what the governing body's role is. Where this is tried it actually seems to reduce complaints.

I am astonished – and heads might do worse than ponder this – by the way in which values which used to be considered the preserve of education professionals have spread into the wider school community of parents and governors, particularly the concern for special educational needs.

Parents want to attend our meetings

I have a tricky question. I am a parent governor in an area such as you often write about, where parents expect their elected representatives to deal with every little dissatisfaction, however personal. You have helped me cope with this, but now I have something new to raise. A number of parents want to 'exercise their right', as they put it, to attend governors' meetings as delegates of the Friends Association. I don't object to this in principle – though I'm not sure that the head and teachers or other governors could be easily persuaded – but I have no doubt that parents' motive is to check up on the quality of representation they get! They often indicate that they expect to know how everybody votes on controversial matters, check that all the points they raise with us are aired, and have full information, not selective, about possible changes to the school, its intake, buildings, staffing, curriculum, before decisions are made. Knowing this, I feel apprehensive. Where do we stand?

Answer

The simple answer is that parents do not have a 'right' to attend governors' meetings at all. *Anyone* has a right to see minutes and papers on any items not classified as confidential, but it is for the governing body *as a whole* to decide to invite non-governors to observe meetings, and in your case it seems quite likely that you won't get general agreement all that easily. I feel mean saying this, because I am in general all for maximum visibility of governors' work, but knowing your problems I share your apprehension about the spirit in which the request is made, and think you may need to do a bit more groundwork on that. I dislike the emphasis on 'checking up' on representatives, and someone does need to get across that you are just that, representatives and not delegates. It is for you alone to judge what is appropriate to raise with the governing body (and even then a majority of your colleagues have to agree) and also how you vote. When I write about oral reporting-back by parent and teacher governors I always emphasise that it is not proper for anyone present to say how individuals voted, and even if a governing body had a very open policy on visitors they might well ask them to withdraw for a vote on something very controversial or a sensitive agenda item. Individual governors should be able to vote conscientiously without pressure. And after all, we don't always know whether a discussion warrants a confidential classification until it has taken place.

There are still some basic things that need to be accepted by your parent body, and I hope your head will continue to support you on this. Firstly they must accept that governors deal with school policies, and not burden their representatives with matters other than those causing *general* concern. (Remember that in a school where there are good arrangements for dealing with individual worries the pressure on governors will be eased.) Secondly they cannot expect you automatically to speak and vote as they dictate, as long as you *report* any widespread concerns, since governors are not 'owned' by their interest group and must vote according to the merits of the case, as they see them, for the school as a whole. Thirdly they must realise that some major changes affecting the school – size, catchment area, staffing, curriculum – need careful, unhurried discussion without excessive pressure, and governors must feel free to explore them fully. But the head should encourage properly structured discussion with parents, and main points of governors' debate should, if not classified confidential, be intelligibly minuted. Obscure minute-writing is no way to keep secrets – it only makes people more determined to get the real story.

Training for support staff governors

As an LEA officer servicing governors, I am being asked how to advise new support staff representatives on their role. Can you please take me through the issues they are likely to raise, so that I can answer questions and plan appropriate training materials?

Answer

Although all governors have the same responsibilities, and the same tightrope to walk between representing a particular interest group and promoting the school's general well-being, I do accept that the new governors we are talking about may encounter particularly difficult problems.

Most obviously, of course, these new governors represent a very wide range of staff. Parent governors and teacher governors have problems often aired in this column, but at least those they represent have something very basic in common, whereas the support staff range from bursars and science technicians to midday supervisors, and in some cases cleaners and kitchen helpers. Any support staff employed by the school can certainly stand for election and vote.

A number of issues follow from this. Firstly the new governors represent a wide variety of people with such different interests that they must be careful not merely to concern themselves with matters relevant to their own jobs, e.g. finance, caretaking, welfare. Secondly, because they may not run into their fellow support staff as often or as naturally as parents meet other parents or teachers other teachers, may even work in different parts of the premises or at different times, they may have to devise some means of getting together before and after governors' meetings to pick up concerns and report back. Thirdly, because they are new and because some of their interests may not yet be regular governors' business, they may at first have to work hard to bring support staff issues into the frame. Finally, because their concerns may have been sidelined by governing bodies in the past, they may need to guard against going to the other extreme, and remember that all governors are there to consider *together* the strategic interests of the school as a whole. If these conflict with a sectional interest the whole school needs come first, and we may all at some time have to accept that something we feel strongly about does not secure general support.

The inclusion of support staff representatives will be welcomed by most other governors, and it will no doubt be stressed in general training and guidance that they are members of the whole school team, making a vital contribution. It would make it easier for them to get involved if, at least for a while, every agenda had a slot for them to report anything of interest or causing anxiety in their 'constituency'. One particular point to mention, however, is that the governing body is not the place for purely workplace grievances – hours, meal breaks, supervision, etc. It would be quite natural for staff to look to their representative to raise these matters for them, but they should be encouraged to go to their line manager or union representative or, in a serious case, think about registering a grievance, in which case governors *would* be concerned.

All concerned should treat these colleagues with respect, encourage them to participate in all activities of the governing body and support them in their representative role. Unfortunately I have had many letters about support staff being wrongly excluded from certain jobs, and not all head teachers are blameless in this – some seem to find the situation difficult. No doubt you will address this problem too.

Part Three:

The Head Teacher and the Governing Body

It's not surprising that so many of the questions I get are about the relationship between the governors and the head teacher. Schools in this country have had governing bodies for centuries, but it's only in the last twenty-five years that their members have been drawn from groups with such an intense interest in doing what the words in their constitution say they are responsible for. In short, the kind of people who became governors before 1980 were rarely any real challenge to the head's authority. The powers of the governing body have in recent years been rather more clearly spelled out too, which to some heads is a provocation.

In other words the conflict, where there is any, is about territory, and arises because the people are different now, as well as the responsibilities more clearly articulated. Year in, year out, it is probably the very commonest issue raised by both governors and heads, and takes two forms. One is that governors misunderstand their role and trespass into the day-by-day management of the school. The other is that heads are not prepared to accept what the law says and spend a lot of energy trying to keep their governing bodies out of their legitimate role. It's as simple as that.

The introduction to Part One of this collection defines the boundaries, and the questions and answers in that section overlap to some extent with the ones reproduced here. But here we concentrate rather more on the occasional, face-to-face, over-the-garden-fence confrontations than the daily goings-on in the beds and borders which get governors into trouble. In this section too we see rather more of the role the good head can have in the daily life of the governing body, as the team-builder and source of inspiration as well as the guardian of territory. Indeed we give pride of place to a newly appointed head who is thinking about these opportunities before even taking up the post. There is no doubt that the best of heads do exercise a leadership role as members of the governing body, not spending precious energy in power games but using the rich resource they have there of varied experience, life-skills and commitment to put their direction of the school on a higher plane altogether. They can, if so motivated, contribute enormously to the smooth working and harmony of the governing body and, through them, to their standing in the community. In so doing they will enhance governors' worth to the school, and provide for themselves as leaders not just a resource but a very necessary support in the relatively new problems of local management of schools, especially the hazards which financial and personnel functions involve. My dream is that this will become the norm, not just an occasional shaft of light like the head who asks that first question I referred to. Here we have a head who approaches the task of building a good governing body with positive feelings, with faith, hope and charity, and who really seems to believe that as a head he will get the governors he deserves.

Yes, of course he is lucky to have a new beginning. But how often is it seen as such? If every time a school got a new head – and think how many will have done so since local management was introduced fifteen years ago – the changeover were seen as an opportunity to develop the governing body rather than display how clever you can be at evading it, what a lot of good energy would be released. Preaching will never achieve that, but perhaps a sympathetic airing, such as I try to achieve, of the issues which cause trouble and how they can be tackled, will bring it nearer. Those who provide leadership training can help, too.

Building a governing body

I am lucky to have been appointed head of a school which over a period is likely to be considerably enlarged and thus recruit extra governors as well as staff. Experienced heads I meet suggest it's very much a matter of luck what sort of governors you get, and perhaps I am being starry-eyed to think a head can have some influence, not direct, of course. But I cling to the hope that a positive approach to the whole business of governors affects the quality of recruits. What do you think?

Answer

I wish there were more like you. You can't have direct influence – or any influence at all overnight – but I too find the fatalistic attitude of many heads to the quality of governors deeply depressing. I really believe as you do that *over a period* the character of the head is a strong influence on recruitment and retention. The best recruiting agency is the reputation of the current governing body, so everything you do as head to influence its self-image, its style, the quality of its work and – vitally – its visibility in the school, will alter the way people perceive it. If the governing body is a pretence it will attract pretenders, if it's a battlefield it will tempt aggressors, if it is a shambles it will recruit muddlers and if it is treated with respect it will attract people worthy of respect.

I mentioned visibility, and if you work to make it a good team, with high expectations, clear aims, good planning and effective working practices, achieving a steadily improving school, I'm sure people will want to join it – *provided they know about it*. Therefore even if all the other conditions are fulfilled, including your own respect for your governors, it's important that what they do is visible, their part in valuable initiatives communicated to parents on a regular basis, and the value *you* place upon their work made explicit. Prospective parent and teacher governors need to see that you accept and support their representative role, and in the case of teachers that you are not too touchy about frank expression of opinions. You'll gain more than you lose from that tolerance.

We should all give realistic guidance about the commitment involved. If people join on the basis that it's a termly meeting and the carol concert, they may not stay that long.But don't forget to say how interesting schools are as well. It's a good idea when you need a new parent governor to let the outgoing one produce a handwritten note (which you copy and send out, of course) to all parents, encouraging them to stand. Remember there are still homes where a formal, typed communication is bad news. And do set up a really well planned and friendly induction process to avoid losing good governors. So many never really bed down because they feel left out of the in-jokes and in-words, the jargon, the relationships, never have anybody they feel free to ask idiot questions of, and so on. All should know whose responsibility it is to provide aspects of that welcome. A proper sequence of help should be offered initially, as well as a display of thoughtful behaviour at the first meeting. The newcomer is invited to attend as many committees and working groups as s/he likes for an introductory period. A mentor for a time is helpful: then it's somebody's job to answer those silly questions so you don't feel bad about asking. Finally, think about team-building. Good teams have a common purpose and talk about it often; have high and explicit expectations of each other on matters like attendance, training, work-sharing and loyalty; and all support each other. Good luck!

> The accountability of professionals to representatives of ordinary people is a feature not just of schools but of all aspects of public life.

A new head wonders whether to become a governor

In the New Year I take up my first headship in a comprehensive. I should welcome any guidance you can give me about starting on the right foot with my governors in general, and in particular about whether to be a governor myself. No one has ever explained the implications to me – though my last head had opted out of the role and would, I'm sure, advise me to maintain my distance as far as possible.

Answer

There is no 'party line' on this subject. A majority of heads do, I understand, choose full governorship, a minority taking your previous head's view. Firstly I hope that whatever you decide, you *will* make up your mind that you are going to work openly, co-operatively and productively with your governors from the beginning. There is no future for the school in armed truce, and indeed all parties, including the pupils, will suffer if there is conflict. The role of governors may change in various ways, but they have been part of the system since the earliest days of education. The accountability of professionals to representatives of ordinary people is a feature not just of schools but of all aspects of public life. The first requirement for harmony therefore is to have respect both for the role itself and the people who fulfil it, and to treat them as equal partners in the strategic management of the school. You, in your responsibility for the day-by-day operation of the school, will find that this acceptance of the partnership, paradoxically perhaps, makes more, not less, likely the sensible acceptance of boundaries. For the rest, I think high and explicit expectations on both sides are vital to this relationship as to most others, and this is worth spending time on. It's also important to start each day afresh; not to overreact to the odd clumsiness or misunderstanding; and to spend some time talking not only about expectations of each other but also about the principles and practice of working together. Find out as much as you can about how your governors have worked together in the past, and encourage discussion of the nuts and bolts of the partnership. I believe that heads who are governors are also better placed to improve teamwork.

You are entitled to attend all governors' meetings, whether or not you are a governor, but as a non-governor you will be a professional adviser rather than a colleague, and strictly speaking, should confine yourself to matters of fact and professional practice. Since you don't have a vote it is not correct to try to influence those who do. (Not all heads who opt out realise or observe this, but it is dangerous not to.) But if you *are* a governor you must, like any other, be loyal to corporate decisions even if you yourself have not been wholeheartedly in support of them. So each choice has its up- and its downside, and the decision individuals make will say a great deal about their attitude to governors. This last may well be a key factor, because the attitude of your governors to your decision could become a very important factor in the relationship. If your predecessor was a governor you may find that governors are uneasy about a successor who isn't. Indeed I think most governors may have this uneasiness and wonder what significance a decision to opt out has for the relationship. So it is a vital decision, and should be discussed more than it is. Should we raise it at interviews?

The critical friend is the governing body, not the individual governor. No school wants up to twenty critical friends all with different points of view, and besides in law only the governing body, not the individual, has any power.

A head who likes office chores

How do we persuade the head to focus on really important matters and keep out of 'technical pursuits' in the realms of ICT, typing and photocopying?

Answer

I wish I had more detail about your problem because there are several hypotheses. Some people do go in for what you might call 'pencil-sharpening' – the things your children do rather than face their homework. I've even known them tidy their rooms when revision calls! It is a common response to either not fancying the important task or not being up to it. If your head is not up to it you have to face the fact that you are paying a big salary to an office assistant, and in an extreme case do something.

But I am not sure that we are on the right track here. Ask yourselves, does your head really spend serious amounts of time on photocopying and other completely mechanical tasks? Because I can see another possible interpretation of the heavy computer use. Coming rather late to modern technology, I've only recently realised how very few people doing high-level strategic jobs today want or need secretarial support as such. They regard their PC as part of their thinking process almost, using a wide range of its capacities. With this proficiency it is quicker even to do your own letters than dictate them, quite apart from exploiting the more sophisticated ways in which technology can support your strategic thinking. If he is one of these, is addressing the major items on the school agenda, not using significant amounts of time on trivialities, but not feeling the need to delegate processes that are like breathing to him, you may be worrying about nothing.

But even if your head is a person of high ability and a wizard with the computer, not simply an overpaid clerk, you may still feel convinced that there are important issues which should be on the agenda of the school and are not. The least hazardous way to approach these may still be concerned questioning by your chair about whether the head could benefit from any more help with routine tasks or more delegation. That should open up the conversation in an unthreatening way, but whoever is to approach him or her must be ready, after some discussion with colleagues, with at least a mental note of some of the issues the school will need to deal with in the coming months, and some idea of how the necessary discussion and sharing with the governing body could be eased. There might, for instance, be a possibility that working with governors on certain subjects could be assigned to an appropriate deputy or other senior colleague. Or it might be that very specific issues could be explored non-committally by small working parties of governors, just gathering information and setting out possible approaches. You must be careful not to give the head the impression that you are trying to usurp his or her leadership role, but properly handled it could lead to a feeling of relief that someone is concerned about the workload and willing to be constructive. Finally, although I sympathise with your frustration, we must remember that the load of responsibility on heads now is colossal and there must be more than one who doesn't know where to start.

A head who turns a school around but has no graces

Three years ago I spoke to you at a conference about our failing school. Inevitably we appointed a new head, and as Chair of Governors I can only marvel at the transformation. The school is now firmly established, not just in recovery but in tip-top performance. The aims were clear, the programme for achieving them precise, good management systems have been put in place, rigorous success criteria established and faithfully monitored. Is everybody happy? In a word, no. Our dear old head valued everybody and gave lots of praise, merited or not. Staff loved him, children loved him, governors got on with him. The new head offends people right left and centre. I don't mind if he recognises himself – he wouldn't care anyway. (It's a matter of 'I didn't get where I am today...' etc.) His manner is brusque, he speaks his mind regardless, he rubs staff and governors up the wrong way and is polite and minimally sociable with parents. I can't fault the way he has turned the school round, but I have already lost a fine colleague from my team, and others talk of resigning. Staff mutter to me every time I show my face. His word is absolute law, nobody else has a role, he gets co-operation, but the muttering increases in volume. Please, what is my role?

Answer

I'm not going to say 'As the Act instructs, you are improving the school's performance', because you know you are doing that and you are not satisfied with it. You know that short-term results can be produced with a mixture of ability, drive and ruthlessness, but you also suspect that without unity of purpose, warmth and appreciation of what others contribute, it may not last. All members of the school team feel good when their efforts get results, but in the long run they will only maintain them if they feel that they are valued and involved. Your head is an identifiable type, encouraged perhaps by the framework we work in, and I would not dispute that after a regime of cosy mediocrity all round some such change may be needed. The skill is in judging the moment to relax the frown and try the smile and the kind word, and you have recognised this. Otherwise the next stage may be that the ablest staff – those who are in a position to go elsewhere as distinct from just suffering it – will move on, that the quality of governors recruited may suffer because it gets round that it's tough going, and maintaining the pace becomes hard work.

I suggest that three people can talk to him. I don't know them so can't say which should take a lead. One is you yourself. You know that. The other is a deputy – you probably know which. The third is your attached inspector/adviser from the LEA. You probably need to talk privately to both these first and sound them out. Then there have to be some frank exchanges about the need for the head to empower a number of other people who are worthy of it, entrusting aspects of the enterprise to them but with the promise of support and appreciation, now that foundations have been laid and bad habits left behind. You must give him full credit for the transformation, but suggest that if it is to be sustained the key players must be empowered and encouraged, and with warmth as well as high expectations. Remember it is a huge challenge to turn round a failing school and takes its toll. He may well be ready to adopt softer techniques and welcome somebody who is brave enough to say when. Good luck.

What price leadership?

Our head – of a primary school in a country town – has recently completed a leadership course designed for head teachers. I don't know what the content was but the effect has been dramatic. He was a pleasant colleague and in most people's estimation an effective leader, but he seems to have gained the impression that he used to be too soft and now has to show muscle. He's completely changed, doesn't listen to staff, dismisses governors' comments as irrelevant, coming as they do from a bunch of amateurs (unless you count a GP and quite a few assorted professionals among our number!), and he wants to introduce an assortment of changes with no consultation. Worst of all there's an air of 'I'm up here and I must be strong' about it. What can we do to restore what was a good relationship?

Answer

I don't know which leadership course this was and very much hope, indeed trust, that it's not typical of the huge variety going on. You've said nothing to suggest that your head was indecisive or vacillating before this road to Damascus experience. I never cease to be surprised by how many people's mental image of leadership is 'out in front' or 'up at the top' when in a school it's so clearly being at the centre, relating appropriately and wisely to a series of overlapping circles of parents, staff, governors, listening and responding to their viewpoints, all with a legitimate bearing on the final decisions, which of course have to be firm and consistent once made, but recognising that they affect a lot of stakeholders. This isn't, I suggest, being weak or trying to please everybody, simply the best way to make sure that decisions when you make them are robust and haven't missed any important arguments.

The relationship you describe with governors is more worrying still, because we are not just there to support decisions already made 'up there' but to provide accountability for the operation of the school. The governing body is also a resource of varied life-experience in different fields, as well as local knowledge, which can be very valuable to an unsure head as yours seems to be. He is unwise to ignore it. I think you need an opportunity to discuss your relationship – preferably off-site and detached from any particular issues – in which you would explore how the legal accountabilities can be made to work, how the lead-up to major decisions should be managed. One point not to be fudged is that heads tend to get the governors their style of leadership deserves, and that in the end the style your head is adopting will produce second-rate support. I am not talking about a social occasion and I think someone from your LEA should be present, either your attached inspector or a senior person from your governor support team. Needless to say, you all, as governors, must be above reproach in not trespassing into legitimate areas of professional authority – day-by-day management of time, space, equipment, staff competence and individual pupil behaviour – which is wrong, and would weaken your case. Your role in these matters comes into play when you decide on curriculum policy, staffing structure, disposition of the budget, behaviour guidelines, in short, a range of basic policies to ensure effectiveness, fairness, consistency, and compliance with the law.

But any rules should express the will of all of you, not a few wishing to put restraints on others.

The worst thing we've ever had to do

Our relationships with the head in this comprehensive school have always been harmonious, but now have reached crisis point. This is because for the first time ever we have overturned a permanent exclusion. I was one of the panel of three experienced governors who formed the discipline committee, under an excellent chair, and we have had a very hard time from the head and are not spoken to by several staff we have been on friendly terms with for years. It is seen as a breach of the relationship. I cannot tell you the detail, but our decision was unanimous, the basis for the exclusion was shaky in the extreme and some of the evidence suspect. Also the school's previous record of support for this student's acknowledged difficulties had not been up to our normal impeccable standard. Our main fear was that the case would not stand up to an external appeal, which would be worse for the school.

Answer

This certainly is the situation every governing body dreads most. Emotions are bound to run high and even the most rational of heads are likely to see it as a betrayal. The staff concerned also feel let down. The fact remains that in carrying out this particular legal process we are there for the child and the family, remembering how serious permanent exclusion will be. We are honour-bound to decide against permanent exclusion if we feel that the offence is not, according to our own guidelines, serious enough; if there is well-founded doubt about the 'guilt' of the student; or about whether, in the period leading up to the incidents, the school has done everything humanly possible to support a student with problems. We also have to look at the evidence, in the light of the possibility of an appeal, and be reasonably sure that a body of independent people will be satisfied. I personally agree that a decision against exclusion by an independent panel is worse for the school, but I have to accept that many professionals don't see it that way and regard a 'hostile' decision by governors as a 'betrayal' – by friends – and, as such, hard to bear.

I assume that you had accepted that the behaviour, if proven, came within the school's published behaviour policy as one meriting permanent exclusion, and the latter was also consistent with the latest government guidance. But you are quite correct in deciding that the evidence also has to be robust and the school's previous record of relevant care acceptable. We owe this to the appellant. I assume too that the LEA representative present did not demur. It's tough – I've come across enough cases to know that. I can only recommend that you remain calm and friendly and don't overreact to the bitter accusations. You will have other opportunities to show your loyalty to the school and your wisdom in dealing with difficult issues, and perhaps professionals will in time appreciate your courage and clear thinking and especially your moderate reaction to their hostility in this difficult case. It might be helpful if the panel offered to meet the teachers mainly involved, with the head, to talk about the need for very robust evidence and the other relevant considerations. But I know you will allow for the intense pressure on teachers in today's secondary schools and the daily contact with challenging behaviour. They do have to think on their feet.

A new PTA and an old-fashioned head

A group of us are very concerned as parents about our brand new school. Naturally we are a close-knit group, pioneers if you like, concerned about many things, especially having had builders on the site for some time after the opening, which gives us serious worries. We have already taken the first steps to form a Parents' Association to discuss matters of common concern. At first the new head said she did not want this but evidently someone in the LEA (ours is very good with parents) put her right, but now that we are drawing up our constitution she is saying it should not be concerned with school policies, as that was for the governing body. But how can our new parent governors take account of our views if we have nowhere to formulate them? The organising group are very happy to fund-raise, and naturally want social events, but I don't think there will be much support if we have no outlet for our small but important concerns, things like drinking water (sometimes turned off), security of the site with builders in and out, and of course mud, as well as learning problems for children who have been moved about a lot.

Answer

Your question sounds like those common forty years ago when PTAs were a novelty, and many of their constitutions did then rule out discussions about educational matters. It's amazing that after all the progress made, with PTAs happily accepted almost everywhere, there is still, as far as I know, no statutory framework for them other than the law applying to charities. But no law can prevent any group from forming an association with whatever legal aims they decide upon, and if they want to meet in the school outside school hours the power to grant that rests with the governing body. No law gives a head teacher the right to forbid it, which doesn't mean that a few won't try to determine its agenda. Obviously you don't want to go ahead without a blessing, though indeed you need the goodwill of all parties. The point you make about parent governors especially needing a mechanism to find out what parents think is a good one, and I hope your governing body will be supportive and able to help you to make your association a success.

You will, I am sure, adopt a friendly tone of voice with the head and bear in mind that life under the conditions you describe is quite hard for her too. But long term you have a role to play in co-operation with your governors to develop a parent-friendly school where reasonable concerns are listened to and taken account of. I agree that this is especially important in a new school, where apart from the passing irritations concerning the building, management has so many decisions to make in a short time about its policies and style. There should ideally be a continuing lively exchange about its development. Make the point that if you don't have a proper structure for this, parents will keep up a barrage of comment as problems arise.

Ideally your constitution should provide for a short meeting of representatives with the head, and with a governor present to listen, at regular intervals, say every half term. Your new head may not feel very confident about such an exchange as yet but it won't be a happy school without it. Neither will fund-raising and social events flourish for long if parents can't also discuss things that concern them, especially in your circumstances. As a first step I should discuss the issue with your parent governors, and if need be the chair, in the light of this reply. If you get the governors on your side it will help. You can tell them that nowadays this is the norm in many schools. If the head can't be persuaded you may have to ask the LEA for support.

> But above all, governors need to build a framework of clear expectations of each other which will, I assure you, change things. When you go into a governing body which has this you can't possibly miss it. It may drive away a few who can't meet the expectations, but those who learn how to do so will be grateful to you because they are no longer outsiders.

Future of permanently excluded pupils

I am chair of the governing body of a comprehensive school. The head and I are very concerned about the enforced admission of pupils from other schools, where the LEA have 'consulted' us but ignored decisions of the full governing body who advised that it was inappropriate to admit these pupils. In two cases we felt that because of problems we had ourselves in the year groups concerned, it would be inconsistent with our duty to all the pupils to accept these pupils (one excluded from a neighbouring school, one from a special school). We fear for the proper exercise of our responsibilities if this continues. Who does control admissions to schools? I am sure others share our concerns.

Answer

As a governor of a comprehensive school myself I can understand your feelings. It is sometimes very hard, especially perhaps when a child with behavioural difficulties has been educated in a special school at primary stage and is judged suitable for mainstream education at secondary age. Many have these concerns. The simple answer to your final question is of course that in a community school the LEA is responsible for *first* admissions, based on a policy on which governors have been consulted, and subsequent individual admissions (e.g. children moving to the area or voluntarily changing schools) are up to the governors, bearing in mind the principles underlying the policy. But when a pupil has been permanently excluded from only one school it is not even within the LEA's control where he or she goes, never mind the governors', because parental choice still applies: if the school has room the governors and the LEA have to admit the pupil. This is the guidance given to all LEAs and reflects the government's policy on parental choice. After two permanent exclusions the parents now forfeit their right of choice, however, and the LEA decides on the placement on the basis of such factors as whether the school has room, its distance from the home, and their view of the child's needs. These are also the considerations in transfers from special schools. I know that some LEAs have in the past used informal committees of governors and heads to advise on these policies and in particular to make sure that schools which happen to have spare places do not suffer unduly and that as far as possible there is fair play between schools. I do not know whether in time the new admissions forums will look at these questions as their role develops, but they are genuinely difficult and I would say that schools which are not full are in the nature of things vulnerable to some degree.

There are certain special circumstances in which a governing body of a community school can appeal against the LEA's decision to admit a pupil excluded from two or more schools, and the Secretary of State may be asked to adjudicate. These include schools in, or just emerging from, special measures; those which have received a warning letter following an inspection; and schools with a very low percentage achieving five A to C grades. The object is to protect schools which are quite likely to have more than their share of problem pupils already.

Exclusion – role of an independent panel

I am a comprehensive head. My governors and I are concerned about a recent appeal against permanent exclusion. Can an independent review panel overturn a permanent exclusion even when the parents have decided that they do not want their child to return to the school concerned? What can this achieve except damage to the school and its reputation?

Answer

Yes, they can decide that the exclusion was not justified, or – I think much more likely – challenge the judgement on which the school based its action in one or more important respects, e.g. that the action might have merited permanent exclusion if deliberate but that there was no evidence of intention to cause the harm which in fact ensued. Parents will sometimes contest an exclusion simply to have the record put straight on something that matters to them. You say that this achieves nothing but damage to the excluding school, but in fact having a son or daughter excluded is a traumatic experience for parents, and if they can wipe out the suggestion of deliberate violence, cruelty or spite, say, or conclude that the school had not done enough to help the child's special problems, it makes it easier to bear, and easier for the new school to accept the child. If they feel that their

69

child has been wrongly accused of deliberate intent to hurt, or was not sympathetically enough handled, it makes it easier to make a fresh start and wipe out the pain that their child's disgrace has caused. Parents who think their child has been treated with unjustified severity may not want a return to the same school anyway, but they do get satisfaction from a public denial of malicious intent. Sometimes it does the excluding school no harm if it makes it doubly careful next time.

Meeting times and a tired head

My school is in a commuter area, and most of my governors either work in town or have partners coming home for an evening meal. All our meetings are at 8.00 pm and there are no regular evenings either for the main governors' meetings or committees. Is this fair to the staff and myself? We have a long day and mostly live too far away to go home first – it is also an expensive area. Nobody will entertain daytime or earlier evening meetings, and the staff who attend and I are exhausted. There is no evening when we can count on going to an evening class or some recreational activity. Any advice?

Answer

I sympathise very much. But we have to remember that governors give their free time voluntarily and that there are bound to be practical limits to what can be done. Also, I think the main governing body meetings should be at a time to suit the non-school-based members. But try a few ideas. It's better to discuss them constructively, rather than as grievances. The first thing is to see if you can find just two days of the week which all can manage for meetings, so that members can safely fit personal needs into the other three. Then I know 7.00 pm wouldn't allow commuters a meal, but couldn't some non-messy food be organised at 7.00? And aim at two hours limit. See if a mixture of day and evening would work – employers are supposed to give reasonable time off for governors' duties and most professional people have a decent leave allowance. Even a small proportion of daytime meetings would give staff a good message. Finally you may find – we do – that people working locally may be willing to come at 8.00 am for anything urgent and we do have a few short meetings at 8.00 or even earlier. If you can squeeze a tolerable mixture out of these options you might find some scope for matching personal interests to committees.

> An individual governor has no authority to challenge or change anything, even if the matter in question is within the governing body's territory.

A disloyal governor

I am the head of a large comprehensive in an affluent area. Our parents are quite demanding – many very ambitious for their children and quite ready to give us a hard time if there's anything they don't like – but we have a mixed intake and of course try to do the best we can for all. Up to now I have worked very well with my governors, who have been supportive and loyal. Sometimes indeed I wish they would challenge us a bit more because it is good for us. But what I cannot cope with is underhand disloyalty and sniping, and I'm afraid one of our new parent governors is spreading very destructive comments among our most sensitive parents. We are thinking we may have to drop Latin next time round because of low uptake, and a few other minority subjects are in danger too – the budget is terribly tight and we are only just making ends meet. We are also talking through a project to restrict the curriculum slightly for a small group of very low-achieving students while they do a day or two of work-related experience every week. All this has been fully aired at governors' meetings and no one has questioned it. This parent has got it into her head that the school is 'going downmarket' and I know she is spreading it around. I don't know how to handle it. Should I confront her before it becomes a bigger problem? Our desire to do the very best we can for able pupils remains unchanged. We operate a lively programme for the gifted, we have a fantastic range of extramural activities and trips, and our options system offers all the choice of academic subjects possible.

Answer

If you are sure this serious gossip is afoot you must first have a talk with your chair. It is better if the chair has a word with any governor who needs guidance rather than the head, and the sooner the better.

But I would first like to put a few tentative questions in your mind about the role your governing body is playing. They are just questions. Don't misunderstand – on the basis of what you have said I am sympathetic, just wondering if any aspect of the professional/governor relationship could be strengthened to make you more secure. You imply the governing body are rather passive – are you sure there is no reluctance to question what you say in a meeting and bring any doubts into the open, doubts, I mean, about the difficulty of maintaining minority subjects, say, and the new work-related curriculum for some? Such reluctance can encourage this sort of 'private enterprise' by the lone parent governor, and your new one is far less dangerous having her say at a meeting. A really detailed and frank debate with all the factors made explicit could give you the chance to ask her specifically what she thinks as well, as a new member. Is plenty of material available for sharing on the arguments for the regular work-experience? Have your *governors* decided on some approximation to a minimum viability group size for low-demand subjects like Latin, say (ours have), and do they know the 'price' of keeping it? Have you yet at least flagged up any topical curriculum/organisation issues in your newsletters to parents? I have always found that in the end the wide sharing of even tentative possibilities reduces rather than feeds destructive gossip, but sometimes only professionals can start the process. Finally, have you explored bidding for all the 'off-ration' sources of funds, e.g. for gifted pupils? I *am* sympathetic – just trying to suggest some countermoves.

Can our head invite visitors to our meetings?

Would you please clarify the question of observers at governors' meetings and committees? This has not been discussed since I was appointed, and I don't know who decides. Once our head invited a head from another school to tell us about an experiment they tried with Key Stage 4 options, which was, I have to say, of great interest, but it didn't seem right for someone to come unannounced. The other thing is that both our deputies attend and play a full part. I'm not saying they should sit like dummies of course, but sometimes they come on a bit heavy on matters where we may not have been in full agreement with the head, and this can be tricky. The male deputy in particular feels he must support the head. We all get on well with each other and the head, and are not afraid of disagreeing, but this could upset the balance.

Answer

Thank you for raising this important issue; you put it very clearly. First, for clarity's sake, I must cover the separate question of non-governors serving on *committees*, who for quite a while have been eligible to serve with voting rights if the full governing body wishes. The governing body must vote each one on individually, saying in each case whether or not they wish them to have voting rights. They cannot be chair or vice-chair, and full governors must always be in a majority when a vote is taken, should that arise. I am not talking here about deputies, who often attend committees which relate to their particular role within the school on a non-voting basis, but the possibility, for example, that the governors might like to co-opt an expert in some relevant field – who could be a staff member – as a visitor with a vote.

That isn't really what you asked, but if I hadn't covered it you might have come across the new rule and been confused. Now for observers proper, at main meetings. The full governing body and only the governing body decides whom to invite as an observer. It is generally considered good practice to invite deputies – maybe in turn, if there's any chance of a power bloc developing, but that's up to you. Not only have they a great deal to contribute from their experience, but I think it is part of our obligation to give them proper professional development in this important dimension.

It is vital, however, that this function remains with the governing body as a whole and that no individual governor, not even the head, casually invites people without consulting. It isn't fair, since nobody would embarrass a visitor by raising the procedural point after the event – it can look as though you are objecting to the person, not the principle. Now that we have to review our committee functions and membership annually, I think we should make the review much more comprehensive and include working practices of all kinds, including policy on visitors. Even if we only confirm existing practice, it makes the point, and it also gives you a chance to be explicit about the role – visitors are welcome to contribute on matters of fact and professional practice, but always bearing in mind that as a non-governor without a vote a visitor must be careful not to take a strong line on a controversial matter, thus influencing those who do have votes. If you have had any serious breaches of this principle I think your chair will have to talk to the head quietly about it and give him the chance to sort it out without embarrassing anyone. If no damage has been done you could settle for covering it in a general review of your working arrangements.

> Inventing or endorsing systems to make things happen or stop things happening can be a major governing body job.

Teachers talking like teenagers

In our comprehensive some of the younger teachers do their best to relate to the teenage culture. I have in mind adopting something like the local accent, touching a kid's new trainers and saying 'Cool, man', even occasionally using really coarse expressions. I know they mean well and often they are the most hard-working and conscientious of our young teachers, but I find it irritates me. Perhaps I'm old-fashioned and feel that teachers should be objects of respect and keep some dignity, though I wasn't aware of that before I started to think about this habit! What do you think? Is it any of our business as governors anyway? Or is it the head's responsibility?

Answer

I know exactly what you mean and it's not uncommon. As you say, it is done with good intentions and often by very caring teachers who want to have the best possible influence. I have come across a few teachers around the country who very naturally slip into the popular idiom, ones not far from their own schooldays but sensitive, and these are often highly successful with the students: their closeness is real but they know the boundaries and don't say anything that a young adult wouldn't naturally say in informal contact. These are also teachers who would not tolerate any speech or action which was unpleasant or coarse, and the students know and respect this so don't take advantage.

I'm afraid I've come across more like the ones you have in mind who put on this act to gain acceptance in the students' world and it can be a miserable failure. Often the idiom is just that bit out of date, or comes over as false, and the students see through it at once. They may privately ridicule it, they may be confused, they may take advantage. Often they are uneasy because they don't know where they stand with the teacher concerned and have a horrible suspicion that he or she will suddenly change tune if they respond too well to the matey approach. In other words, it's counterproductive. If it comes naturally and is convincing, fine. But peripheral – what children and adolescents most respect is fairness, enthusiasm, well-prepared and interesting lessons and conscientious attention to their learning needs. If all this is combined with real understanding of their feelings and aspirations the teacher is winning, but there are few shortcuts. I'm not sure that they want adults to enter their world through shortcuts anyway.

As to whether it's governors' business, I would say on the whole no, not directly anyway. The head is the person to set standards of teacher styles and behaviour, and a wise one can accommodate many styles within a general culture of mutual respect. He or she is also the one to 'have a word' if someone's style is markedly unsuitable. It's the sort of thing a chair with a really close relationship with the head could mention informally, but no more. Your best influence as governors is through the aims and ethos of the school, where you can cover relationships between adults and students and how a mutually respecting culture is created: ideally this will be reflected in the staff code. You will also come up against this issue sometimes in interviewing candidates for posts or promotion, and it could be quite a revealing topic if your senior management think it's important. In the end I suppose we should all remember that there are many kinds of good teacher and that students as well as their seniors will be able to see through any veneer the real foundations of respect between the generations.

Please help us out of this quagmire

I am the longest serving teacher, other than the deputy head, in this primary school. I see it drifting into destructive conflict and realise how powerless a teacher is. Our head has his strong points, but has never accepted the more open habits now required of schools. He avoids any debate about school policies, panics into secrecy over anything controversial, refuses to discuss complaints, keeps parent in the dark and – of course! – handles governors badly. The atmosphere is terrible. An opinionated political governor feels the school could do much better (and our OfSTED wasn't brilliant) and an overenthusiastic parent governor acts as the watchdog for all parents' interests and their main communicators – holding her own consultations, making long reports, badgering head and teachers with both individual and general complaints, etc. These two absolutely dominate. I wonder if I dare intervene. I know all this is so common that I don't even fear being identified. The head gets more and more unreasonable and paints himself into corners, the teachers are full of foreboding. It isn't a bad school and has no really serious problems, yet the atmosphere is one of impending crisis. The parent governor is desperate and talks of moving her children, and next term we enter the minefield of mixed age classes because budget constraints mean we must lose a teacher.

Answer

You are right, it is a classic, and I could be accused of inventing it as a case study! I also agree that in many schools teachers have little chance to influence really bad situations, and you certainly can't intervene in meetings. The two people who could – given the paralysis which afflicts the head – you don't mention. These are the chair and the teacher governor/s. And possibly at a personal level the deputy head could influence the head. I suppose it's asking a lot of the teacher governor/s to try to move the protagonists to the middle ground where (i) governors recognise that they can only act together to solve school problems; (ii) the head accepts that the governing body has a right to know and discuss all important matters; (iii) all realise that parents *will* bombard their governors with concerns if the school does not deal with them properly itself; and (iv) all governors and particularly parent governors take parents' information needs seriously. But when teachers are so distressed by the situation, a good teacher governor has a duty at least to warn fellow governors. The other powerful person is the chair, who must, from all you say, be weak. The chair should stand up for the governing body's right to concern itself with school standards and parents' perceptions, and also rein back any 'overenthusiastic' members. He or she might well also counsel the head privately about his failure to communicate, about the dread mixed age classes especially. You are right – this will be a flashpoint, and parents will go through the roof if not carefully handled.

Although you have no official role, do you not feel able, with your long service, either to talk to the head on these lines, or at least convey through your teacher governor the need for an effective chair? Can your LEA training team (or attached inspector, who also might be able to influence the head) not give you an in-house session on roles and responsibilities? I know from experience that schools which do not communicate properly with parents at a professional level will almost always develop dysfunctional governing bodies, and often find themselves in crisis.

A man of strong dislikes

Our head has many fine qualities. He is wise, energetic, he cares passionately about the school and all the children, whatever their ability and background, and is great with parents. There's just one thing that bothers us. He takes strong and seemingly irrational dislikes to a number of staff members. We have a staff of 65 or so and it seems that at any time about a dozen are in his bad books. He'll complain to any passing governor, but especially the chair, that this one and that one are bone idle, insolent, useless, or even Welsh. As far as we can tell he doesn't act on these prejudices and the hit list does change almost weekly. I don't suppose you have any experience of this sort of thing, but any advice would be welcome. We are very conscious of the responsibility such a large staff represents.

Answer

No, I haven't experienced this personally, but from listening around I don't think it's all that uncommon. It's indiscreet and it's not pleasant (especially the bit about the Welsh, which I take personally!) but I suspect that for a few people it may be no more than a way of releasing tension. Considering the number of people they employ, schools are very tight communities where tensions build up and break up all the time, and we all know the stress level in schools can be high. If your head is such a paragon I'd be surprised if this goes deep, especially as you imply that it is a fluid hit list. He obviously feels very at ease with your chair (which is a good thing) and he may even be winding him up a bit, in which case a similarly light rebuke might be the right response. You were careful not to say or hint that it affected any action or official judgement this head makes about people. It would be serious if the hit-list candidates of the moment were treated badly or the regular victims failed to progress in their careers. In this case I think your chair would have to speak to the head very seriously and express the concern of the rest of you. My instinct is that it is superficial, maybe even half-joking, a tension-releaser – but dangerous all the same, and worth a friendly warning. I attach great importance to governing bodies keeping an eye on processes in which fairness can be infringed – job adverts, vacancy notices (especially internal) and job descriptions – for any sign of partiality. Note that the latest regulations, which exclude us from the appointments procedure below deputy level, still refer to our having a role in job descriptions. And remember, we remain responsible in law even without a say in the choice of candidates.

> If as a head you believe your governors are incapable of contributing anything, I'm afraid it is very likely that what has happened to them *is* your fault.

Our head speaks disparagingly of us

We know that our head (who is a governor) speaks very rudely about the governing body and individual members, especially in the staffroom – and he has enough enemies there to ensure that it gets back. He has also, we understand, said these things in meetings with other heads, LEA officers, etc. He criticises not just our judgement but our lack of education, speech, etc. Are we wrong to get upset?

Answer

Certainly not, and you must act, if only to protect this offender, little as he deserves it. I'm glad you told me he was a governor – even if he were not it would be intolerable, but if he has the privileges of governorship he is obliged to be loyal and discreet, like the rest of us. I knew of a head who came very close to losing his job because he spoke disparagingly of his governors and their majority decisions at other meetings, and in the pub. Corporate responsibility is a basic requirement.

We can't get governors of the right quality

I'm a brand new head – well almost – in a decent, drab, working-class estate, and mostly this is where our children come from. There is a lot of parental interest and involvement, however, nurtured by my predecessor, and tremendous commitment to the school and concern that children should do well. I value this and hope to keep it. It's the governors who worry me. There's no problem getting them. Parent elections were, as always, strongly contested this term, we never have vacancies, though we don't attract any bank managers or the like, and from first impressions I have to say that the governors are thoroughly nice people, conscientious, sensible, wanting to help. If I wanted a brick barbecue built or a door

hung the other way they'd all be queuing up. But honestly, they haven't
the education to cope with the kind of issues we have to address, they
are baffled by educational terms and the abstractions we deal in, and I
defy anyone to overcome that. I always thought it was madness to give
governors these responsibilities, but at least in your leafy suburb you
might get the odd somebody. Can you please reply, if only to tell me I'm
a terrible snob.

Answer

Yes, you're a terrible snob. But I think you expect me to say more than that. So
I'll start by saying that many heads would give their eyes for the interest and
commitment your school attracts, and I'm afraid you *will* lose it if you let your
lack of respect for these people show. Many heads in leafy suburbs would gladly
swop a few somebodies for a few of yours too, if my post is anything to go by.

You really are lucky to have governors who volunteer, who care and want to learn,
and I wouldn't underestimate the intelligence needed to hang a door the other way
either. One of the most impressive governors I ever knew, one of the earliest
parent governors to be elected years before they were legally required, could hang
a door the other way and assemble a flat-pack while we egg-heads were trying to
understand the instructions! He wasn't too hot in the reading and writing
department. He did knock us out of bed after midnight once to tell me they'd just
made a disastrous head teacher appointment, and he couldn't have been more
right, as it turned out, or a few somebodies more wrong. He also knew why he
was worried, but had not the code to express it, and he gave me a salutary lesson
in not underestimating people, as well as the need for inclusive language.

Please believe that from my experience governors who know the long words don't
have a monopoly of understanding or judgement, and you will be well rewarded if
you can engage the interest and understanding of yours as well as their goodwill.
It's often said that the issues governors confront are difficult to understand, but I
think they rarely are. It's the code they are presented in which is so often
impossible, and we shall all have to get a lot better at putting simply the things we
have to decide, without being affected or patronising, if we are to get the best out
of the raw material each community offers. It can also be an aid to clear thinking.
So many 'decent, drab areas' can't easily get governors at all. You have worked
miracles in yours – don't throw them away.

> Please believe that from my experience governors who know the long
> words don't have a monopoly of understanding or judgement.

Are results all that matter?

We had a new head in September 2000. The previous one retired early following criticisms about the performance of the school, which nearly ruined her health. I have to say that it was a happy place both for pupils and staff, and that is no longer so. The staff feel that they are being chased the whole time, the smallest faults being picked on. Discipline of children is also, I think, heavy, parents don't seem to come in to help any more and clearly don't feel welcome, and the relationship with governors is dire. We get very little information, are expected to rubber stamp things without any background, and the most innocent question or comment produces a snappy response. The head clearly thinks we are a waste of time at best and at worst a hindrance to her school improvement plan. There is no point in going on and I am writing to you as a last hope before resigning, though this makes me sad, as I am very committed. Now here's the punch line – the SATs results and other indications of performance have much improved and that is what we all want. But is it only possible at such a price?

Answer

Your question made me think, as you can imagine. No, of course I don't believe that performance can only improve at the expense of relationships, and I would take a lot of convincing that a school where relationships with staff, children and parents are poor and where governors are not allowed to perform their legal function, can thrive in the long term. A short, sharp shock may produce temporary results but in the end the foundations have to be sound. If you have the heart for it you must go on trying to strengthen those foundations.

You have told me a great deal but the crucial thing missing is why the school was underperforming before 2000. The previous head is the key to understanding that. It's possible to be a lovely person and create a good atmosphere around you without having the slightest notion of how to manage a complex institution, get the best out of staff and pupils, and engage governors in a productive dialogue about the knobs and levers which make up a strategic improvement plan. However nice your old head was, you have to accept that she didn't have those skills, and I think governors should be reflecting on this and also asking themselves whether *they* might have identified the critical missing factors. Only this will help you to talk about how you can contribute to making the improvement lasting and at the same time try to ensure that the price tag isn't so impossibly high.

I have nowhere to look for clues, but there is bound to have been an OfSTED report at some time, or an LEA inspection which judged the school to be underperforming. Low expectations are a likely answer and often afflict a friendly and easy-to-please person. You should search just as hard for the detail of what has been done in two years to bring change about. But also someone – your chair, a deputy. a close and trusted member of staff, your attached LEA inspector or governor training officer – *must* talk to the head about her style, the proper role of governors and the importance of winning parents' and children's confidence, and of course, above all, that of staff. Two things I'm sure about and I hope I've made them clear. One is that you can't create lasting school improvement just by being nasty, and the other that you don't produce failure simply by being too nice. You must look deeper for the other factors.

Should the head patronise us in this way?

This is quite a poor area where few people have had the privilege of higher education, but as one of the lucky ones I dislike the patronising way the head talks to, and about, the governors generally. They elected me chair because nobody else felt confident enough to take it on, but they are a wonderful lot of people and I feel privileged to work with them – sensible, will do anything for the school, care passionately about the children. I have no problem, left to myself, in working with any of them. They understand the issues that come before us perfectly well and make wise contributions, though they sometimes need a little help putting their thoughts into the right words.

The trouble is that often I'm not *'left to myself'. The head tries to draw me into his attitudes, and wants to conspire with me, if I can put it that strongly, to bypass the rest whenever possible on the ground that they aren't able to grasp the difficult matters we have to deal with. He mostly wants me to talk things through with him and then draft something which we can put to governors for approval, making it clear to them that he thinks they need this 'support'. I feel this puts me in a false position.*

Answer

How lucky the rest of your colleagues are to have you. That's the first thing I must say, since whatever it looks like you do respect them and want to work with their full participation. But what it looks like *is* important – and dangerous. Yours isn't the only head who finds it easier to work closely with the chair and present the other governors with drafts and policies to rubber-stamp. Many do it even where there can be no doubt about the majority's understanding of the issues, and it not only usurps the corporate authority of the governing body but puts everyone in real danger. When worms turn they can upset the best-laid plans.

I believe you when you say that your governors have no difficulty understanding the issues. One doesn't need higher education to grasp the typical problems governing bodies face. I have never found lack of understanding to be a problem. Some people in senior positions write in words which disguise meaning and may exclude those whose world doesn't begin and end with words, and they are immature. But they often succeed in undermining readers' self-confidence. Only you can stop this happening, and you must have the courage to resist being drawn into a false relationship which excludes others. All policy issues should go directly to the governing body for discussion, and you must take every opportunity to indicate to the head and your colleagues that you think them capable of this.

But words alone won't raise their self-esteem. The next thing is to organise them into committees, working parties or drafting groups to tackle issues and needs that are still on the horizon, and make sure your head flags such issues and needs in his reports. Take care that they always get papers in time, not at the meeting, and go round the table before you assume agreement on any issue. You might like to give individuals an issue to present in turns, and move as soon as you can to getting some teachers routinely into governors' meetings and governors into teachers' meetings to brainstorm policy at early stages. They will soon gain confidence *if* – and it's a vital if – you never fail to show your own respect for them and your faith in their ability.

Building a relationship with a new head

Our previous head and later the acting head who had been under his influence were what you would call 'territorial' – unwilling to accept that we had any serious part to play. We are most anxious to make a good start with the new head who has just taken up his post, but beginning with an ultimatum hardly seems the right prescription.

Answer

I agree no ultimatum. But it's a shame not to take advantage of a fresh start. The first thing to say is that I very much hope that you have already laid good foundations through the selection process. The panel of governors you elected to carry out the shortlisting and interviewing surely, in the circumstances, put the need to find a governor-friendly candidate pretty high on their agenda, and I should be surprised if you hadn't all discussed beforehand how you were going to find out what candidates' approach to governors would be. Of course I know some are 'April when they woo, December when they wed', but even so the dialogue you had then is a kind of unwritten contract which you must not allow to be forgotten: things will never be the same as they would be if you hadn't had that conversation. So do show in casual ways that you remember.

You must talk with your head *now* about general working-together issues. The new Regulations recently made under the 2002 Act give you an ideal excuse to have a session with him in which you first run through the responsibilities of governors as laid down in the Act itself. Look particularly at Section 21, which says that, subject to any contrary provisions, 'the conduct of the school shall be under the general direction of the governing body', and that the latter shall conduct the school 'with a view to promoting high standards of educational achievement'. Then you can look at the issues raised by the large batch of regulations made under it (September 2003), dealing, for instance, with what you should decide the size and composition of your governing body might be, what it delegates to committees or the head, and the implications of these choices for open and participatory working together. I warn you that in the wrong hands these possibilities could be used to just the opposite effect.

Then, either on the spot or at some planned future date, you should talk as a group with the head about the kind of strategic information you need to have routinely so that you can keep yourselves informed of the school's work and life. It is particularly important to discuss the timing of consultation with governors, and ask your new head if in his report to you at meetings he could, in addition to informing you of recent developments, flag up coming events, key dates, expected circulars, anything, in short, which will require a decision from governors, so that you can plan your involvement, meeting dates, etc., and not always be in a position where you are asked to approve decisions too late to change. For the same reason, emphasise how highly desirable it is that governors should be aware of important changes at the brainstorming stage.

Lose no opportunity to remind senior management of the need to involve you in a meaningful way. Always be pleasant, *expecting* that the right things will be done. The first meeting of the year is a great opportunity to get things on the right footing – and most of us waste it.

Do we have to give our head an annual rise?

This is not an easy thing to say, but I am unhappy about the pressure our head always puts on us when the annual salary review comes up. It is not exactly intimidating, but there is a strong feeling that if we don't agree an increase it is a vote of censure or at the very least shows a lack of appreciation. We do appreciate our head, who is very efficient and hard-working, but our budget is tight and I feel we need some special reason.

Answer

You put very clearly an issue which a number of governors have raised with me. Hard as it is, we must be clear and firm about it. It was never intended that heads' salaries should rise automatically each year. We exercise discretion in fixing the head's pay on appointment, and often do so above the minimum in the salary band for our size of school to take account of the character of the catchment area, any difficulty in filling the post, and so on. Increases can be given in circumstances on which we have clear guidance and we must follow this carefully when we set our targets and later assess whether they have been met. I am not suggesting that we shouldn't take other more general aspects of leadership into account, but unless there is a reason over and above that the head is doing an effective job, it is very wrong for him to put you in this situation. It has become a major unspoken resentment among governors in too many schools of late and needs expressing. All credit to the many heads who wouldn't dream of exploiting the governor relationship in this way.

Some people in senior positions write in words which disguise meaning and may exclude those whose world doesn't begin and end with words; they are immature.

... and a head teacher's view on pay

I was concerned by your answer on heads who ask for a pay rise. It is heads who should resent having to go cap in hand to a group of people who are often complete amateurs, and are then made to feel guilty for asking. If governors can't cope with this job, that's their problem. We may even have people who work for us determining policy, if not individual salaries, on pay committees.

Answer

I think you speak for many head teachers. But I was also responding to many governors who, having judged that there is no case for an increase within the rules, feel embarrassed by having to refuse. It isn't a pleasant situation and I'm sure I'm not the only governor who, given a choice, would sooner not have that particular job, though I have to admit that it probably goes logically with the other roles we have. All I was trying to say is that we are doing the job the law has given us and within the criteria laid down, and those criteria don't provide for *automatic* increases. Therefore, if a head asks for an increase with targets perhaps not met and no obvious change in the situation to warrant it, governors feel bad.

I cannot, however, let your remarks about 'amateurs' and 'people who work for you' go unchallenged. The misconceptions behind these words are widespread, and lie at the heart of many poor relationships. The fact is that every expert who does a job in our society is in some way answerable either to a client or to a body of representative non-experts. A school governor is no different from a magistrate, a juror, an MP, local councillor, member of a health authority or a non-executive company director. All in some sense make serious decisions on behalf of the community or undertaking. They have experts to advise them and experts to carry out their decisions. But they themselves have this role by virtue of representing ordinary people and the community's or shareholders' interest in certain activities.

As for staff governors, the law has decreed that staff should contribute to the range of interests and opinions brought to bear on governing schools. It also makes it clear that they may only be kept out of particular activities if they stand to gain personally from the outcome. They are entitled to serve on pay committees if their colleagues so decide, but not to discuss salaries of individuals.

> The special concern of community governors should be the school's impact on members of the wider public – their safety, peace, space, amenities; the effect of school plans on land use; its pupils' behaviour outside school; its relationship with householders, the elderly, local shops. But once more, all points of view should be heard, and if there is conflict, the school's interest comes first.

Responsibility for senior management weaknesses

I suppose you'd call me a dinosaur among heads, if that means having had my formative experience in very different times and finding it hard to adapt. My country town comprehensive still has a few of the staff we opened with after a reorganisation twenty years ago, when I was senior master. Since becoming head I have tried to value people, which I still think gets results. I also try to make allowances for any who are going through bad patches and have learned to work around them. I think I have influenced in the same tradition those who have stayed with us, and they accept that sometimes weaker colleagues have to be carried. The result is that I have one deputy and perhaps two departmental heads who are not working to the highest standard and in my view never will. We manage, and it is a caring and happy school.

Following our OfSTED report, which was not good, I have been under considerable pressure from governors, encouraged by the LEA, and clearly I am thought to have shown weaknesses in leadership. I suspect there is a move to force me into early retirement. Can I really be held responsible for colleagues whom I have tried in vain to support? After all, teaching is not a job where people are put on the pavement without warning with their belongings thrown after them. What could I have done, even had I been that sort? And why don't people understand that I go the extra mile myself to avoid what I consider draconian policies?

Answer

I understand your feelings. But twenty years ago the governors, with the head, did not have the same total responsibility, and going the extra mile could be enough. The head is now fully accountable to the governors not only for the total quality of the school's teaching and learning, including the performance of team members, but also for spending the budget available to the very best advantage. This accountability will be seen to cover the communication of high expectations, the setting of targets, counselling, professional development, and, in the last resort, a judgement as to whether the best that a staff member can do is good enough.

It's true that you can't put teachers on the pavement with their belongings, and I would never want to see such a possibility. There is a very long road, and a series of fair and careful steps along it, to be travelled first. If you have never transmitted high expectations, set targets, given guidance, organised professional development, then I'm afraid that by present standards you *have* failed to provide leadership. The fact that you have worked so hard yourself to make up for the shortcomings of others must be advanced in mitigation, but these days the total responsibility you have for managing the institution, not just the teaching, means that every penny invisibly spent on less competent staff comes out of the total available to spend on the children.

Your governors haven't come out of it very well either if, as I suspect, they have waited for the clear signal from OfSTED before intervening. I do know that some governing bodies try in vain to give warning signals but stop short of plain speaking, especially if they admire the dedicated head. So these may fail to make progress, even if they have the information to judge. It sounds as if there may still be time to save the situation, but only if you accept that the new freedom that schools – and heads – have to run the show does also carry a much bigger responsibility for the performance of everybody in it. I hope your governors, when you have made this adjustment, will support you in what needs to be done, and that it doesn't have to be extreme.

How can we tackle our head's unacceptable behaviour?

I am a parent governor, fairly new, in this Church of England School. I knew before I took on the job that it had become a very unhappy school since the appointment of the current head. She has a lot of friends in high places, I understand, both the LEA and the church, but surely she shouldn't be bomb-proof. The trouble is her bullying style, which everyone knows about and nobody tackles. Our teacher turnover is high and several teachers have been off with illnesses due to stress. At least half the teachers regularly approach individual governors in tears, talking about how cruelly they are treated, and several have already come to my house. I have talked to our chairman but he is a peace-at-any-price sort and says there is nothing we can do, and that teachers are always whingeing. Some other governors are as worried as I am but bewildered about how they can help. One has talked to the vicar, another to an LEA personnel officer he plays golf with, but nobody has an answer. Yet from our governing body meetings you'd never think anything was wrong.

Answer

Yours is a classic malfunctioning governing body, even to the telltale fantasy quality of its meetings. What you do together bears no relation at all to what as individuals you perceive to be problems. You tell me about this one approaching the vicar and that one approaching the LEA, about individual teachers crying on your shoulders, etc. You are all very well motivated, but the hardest lesson is that individual governors who try to take up a problem themselves always come to grief, and if it involves teachers being encouraged in the kind of confidences you describe, they suffer too. It is all unstructured, unscientific, and changes nothing. Yet you clearly have a serious problem which only the governing body acting together can solve.

I do sympathise with teachers who have to spend their working lives in the way you describe. But it doesn't help them at all to pour it out to individual governors who because of diffidence or fear of litigation don't – can't – take it any further except in whispers, and would only do the teacher concerned further harm if they did, so what's the point? Whatever problems teachers have, there is some proper process for it within their workplace. It may mean initially – depending on the subject – going either to their line manager, their union, their teacher governors or, formally, their governing body. In your situation it seems quite likely that they have a case for acting together as a group to bring a grievance case, which would be handled by a committee of governors, with an appeal panel of different governors no less in number than the original committee. The investigation would be thorough, objective, and hopefully constructive. It doesn't have to end in the dreaded outcome. Often a professionally conducted enquiry can help the person complained of to identify and cope with problems which are holding him or her back and create a fresh start. Get guidance from your LEA on procedures by all means when the time comes, but accept that it is your responsibility as a group to handle the issue.

It sounds as if your chair is short on leadership quality. The rest of you may need to put these points forcibly to him. There is a new procedure for voting a chair out of office in the last resort, with very strict safeguards to ensure fairness. But be sure that he isn't saveable with better support and also, if it comes to the crunch, that a heavy majority will stick together and that you can make your concerns stick.

> The governing body is not there to manage teachers or teaching. It is there to provide the best possible environment for teaching and learning, to establish a framework of policy and principle within which teachers can work effectively, to establish sound and equitable systems for that work to be checked, encouraged and further developed. It is the job of professionals – subject leaders and ultimately the head teacher – to check the work of individual teachers, to advise them and develop their skills.

Part Four:

Working Together

T his section covers a wide range of issues, many of them of great importance to governors. Where it inevitably overlaps with other sections – for example on boundaries, on representative roles, and on head teacher's responsibilities, it is because the question or the answer, or both, also have a strong element of active team-building, decision making, or honourable behaviour within the group, whatever their source. More obvious issues of teamwork are also strongly represented, with questions on rules and procedures, good practice, chairing skills and pitfalls, dealing with difficult colleagues and making sound decisions.

Probably the most difficult lesson first-time governors have to learn is that they have no power as individuals. The only legal authority belongs to the governing body, and this is often frustrating in the context of individuals' representative role, because they cannot always deliver what their group desire. Individuals contribute from their varied experience and knowledge – and prejudices! – and this is the richness of the structure, but in the end the product is a decision democratically arrived at which may alter for good or ill the service provided for children and their families. This highlights the importance of good teamwork and efficient working arrangements, tolerance of others, sound relationships and skilled chairing.

The role of the chair, indeed, is a strong theme in this section. There can be few other bodies in which the chairperson has so little personal power but such tremendous personal influence. Although the scope for delegation has been greatly increased, not all governing bodies will use it extensively, and without a specific mandate the chair has no power to act without authority except in a dire emergency. This makes his or her task of establishing good and equal relationships among governors, and ensuring that their discussions are purposeful and their decisions firm and clear, a very difficult one. He or she also has to maintain a supportive relationship with the head without compromising the role of the governing body. Among governors the chair must try to ensure that powerful individuals do not dominate and that there is no tendency for 'A and B teams' to develop.

The head teacher too has a major role in promoting good teamwork, harmony and effectiveness on the governing body. It is a wise head who gives this aspect of the work deep thought as soon as he or she is appointed, because early mistakes may be hard to live down and first impressions on an inevitably anxious governing body are lasting. For this reason wise heads when established in the post will give deputies plenty of opportunity to become familiar with governors' work so that they are not at sea when their turn for headship comes. New heads also have to think carefully about whether or not to be governors, since this decision not only strongly affects their ability to influence members, but also how governors regard them. The implications of this choice are discussed in this section.

Proper observance of roles and boundaries, understanding the limits of the representative role, correct observance of rules and procedures, all play their part in an effective governing body. Perhaps most crucial of all, however, is the governing body's acceptance of the equal value of every member, so that there is no domination by powerful individuals, no A and B teams, no attempts to subvert the rules in order to produce a particular outcome. To such a fortunate governing body, work-sharing, honest and open discussion, and concentration at all times on the best outcome for the pupils, will come naturally.

Who decides procedural questions?

Can you clarify some procedural matters where a lot of influence seems to rest with the head in our school? First, the timing of meetings. These are in effect laid down by the head, and take little account of the convenience of volunteers who also have their livings to earn. Who decides? Second, the agenda. The head and chair put it together, and if a governor suggests an item, as often as not it is ruled out as inappropriate, or postponed. Third, issues about what particular governors can take part in. The head, for instance, has ruled that the only people helping with teacher appointments should be those with outside experience of interviewing. (I know this involvement won't be happening anyway after this term but I just wanted to illustrate his attitude.) Parent governors are often excluded from discussions because they have a child affected. Teachers are told they must clear any expression of views with him in advance, and support staff governors have been told they cannot be on committees. Sometimes the head will say that a governor has a conflict of interest and must withdraw.

Answer

Your head is certainly taking more upon himself than is proper, but perhaps the governing body is not sufficiently confident to take responsibility. First, timing of meetings. The *whole governing body* should discuss and decide what is best for the majority, trying not to disadvantage anyone or any group. But obviously decisions must be fair to those governors who work in the school as well as those whose livings are earned elsewhere. For instance, you can't always have meetings in school time or, I would say, straight after school, but I would also think it unreasonable to have them all at 8.30 pm, say, since an area where many governors commute (and would appreciate being able to have something to eat before they go out) may also be just the sort of area where teachers live far away from school and would just have to hang around for hours, making a long day.

Compromise is needed, and possibly a mixture of times adopted, to take account of all members' needs. In evening meetings arranging a few sandwiches would be thoughtful too. I heard of one LEA who gave teacher governors an allowance to spend on a meal or transport home and back.

Formally you all decide on the agenda, and though in practice a small group must plan it, you must ensure that no reasonable item is excluded, discussing disputed cases if need be. On governor involvement in general duties and decisions it is the whole governing body which decides, not the head, and in a case where there might be a conflict of interest affecting any governor, it is again the governors, not the head, who make the judgement. I would certainly not think having a child in a class affected by a decision would count. The whole governing body should also protect its members against excessive restriction. It is very wrong to exclude staff governors from any normal duties. The only things employees of the school can't do are take the chair and participate in decisions on a colleague's appraisal or pay. Trying to muzzle teacher governors is slightly different, in that although it is extremely bad practice and conflicts with the principle of equal right to participate, it usually takes place in private and is difficult to stop. But the rest of the governors should encourage teacher colleagues to contribute freely and support them if there is evidence that they suffer for it. The practice impoverishes the governing body's discussions, and discourages good candidates. You could say heads get the teacher governors they deserve.

> It's often said that the issues governors confront are difficult to understand, but I think they rarely are. It's the code they are presented in which is so often impossible.

Shouldn't all governors have the chance to put an item on the agenda?

Some of us – especially the parent group – feel excluded from any real say in the work of the governing body, which after all is determined by what is on the agenda. This just appears – I don't know from where – and the only times my particular friends and I have asked for something to be discussed we have not been successful. This makes us feel we are being muzzled and that perhaps the things we want debated would upset somebody's applecart. You often talk about A and B teams, and 'censorship by agenda' seems to be the main way in which some members get to be 'more equal than others'. I genuinely don't know how the agenda is decided, and governing bodies will never be truly democratic until everyone has the same right to suggest matters to discuss.

Answer

This is a very good question and many governors will echo your sentiments. I do have some suggestions for change but first may I dispose of what may be misunderstandings?

I know that any group may contain people who would like to control the agenda, but I don't really think that this whole agenda business is a deliberate conspiracy against democracy – which isn't to say that it's working well. We have to decide the agenda in advance – otherwise no preparation of papers or thinking about issues can take place. But you can't have as many as twenty people meeting just to decide what they are going to discuss when they meet, neither can you accept extra items on the night unless they are urgent because (a) you'd run out of time and (b) nobody would have had a chance to think at their own speed about them – which isn't very democratic either. So you need a mechanism in the form of a small group who will meet beforehand – and the obvious nucleus are head, chair and clerk – to draw up an agenda, and this is exactly what happens in most schools. This agenda will in fact contain a few things which are 'regulars' (apologies, head's report), a few which come up because of the time of year (election of chair, exam results, entry numbers), and a few arising from national or LEA initiatives. Anyone is at liberty to make suggestions – if they know when and to whom, and that's the first thing to put right with regular reminders – but there is no clear right to have those suggestions accepted other than by general agreement on the night. Now that's really quite democratic, because the decision can in theory be the whole governing body's, but the snag is, it may not be practical to squeeze it in that meeting and the next may be too late. Also individuals will not have time to think through the issues beforehand.

So firstly a school needs to publicise the fact that a group meets and will consider suggestions for the agenda by a certain date. That alone won't prevent what you suffer from but it's a start. Then I think in a perfect world there ought to be a national rule that any three governors have a right to put an item on if they ask in time. That is in line with the existing rule that any three can actually arrange a special meeting – which is a much more significant right – and it is also a safeguard against hobbyhorses. The Government doesn't seem to have been keen on that idea, but in the new permissive atmosphere of 2003–4 I really don't see why any governing body can't adopt it as a policy of its own if it wishes. One warning. If you want to suggest an arrangement like this on your own governing body, it's important that small groups don't use it to get the governing body discussing concerns affecting individual children or families, the sort of issue all parent governors get thrust at them every time they go out. They should be genuine issues of school policy which are suitable for discussion in a policy-making body.

Can we co-opt our caretaker?

Agroup of us talked about the constitution regulations (2003 No. 388) and what changes we may want to make. We think smaller governing bodies are more efficient and when we reconstitute ours we are very unlikely to go above a membership of twelve. We know we will have to have at least four parents and two LEA reps but we don't want more than two elected staff even if allowed. This is because we'd really like to go to four co-options (which already makes twelve). There are a couple of local organisations who would expect to be represented and we also need someone from business, but we really do want to have our caretaker who knows all about the lettings, etc. and is a vital member of the school team. We wondered whether, if we co-opted him now before we reorganise, he could stay on, or alternatively could we keep one of or co-opted places for him? Mind you, our head is against having the caretaker on at all because he is a bit outspoken, but he knows I am writing to you and will abide by what you say. We already have our school secretary – whom the head likes, I guess – on our board now, so what's the difference?

Answer

I'm glad you are getting on with your thinking about reconstitution even though it doesn't have to be complete until 2006! I'm sure you've heard me say how concerned I would be about a medium to large school going for too small a governing body, simply because the other new regulations (2003 No. 1377), which came into force in September 2003, allow so much more delegation to committees and individuals. If numbers are small and balance suffers there may be some risk of A and B teams.

But that's another issue. I'm afraid you can't co-opt your caretaker either now or when you have reconstituted. Co-option of school staff was stopped when staff got their own elected representative under the 1999 Act (presumably your school secretary was elected) and in fact the 2003 regulations go much further and say that no staff can serve in any capacity other than elected staff governors. They can't be parent governors in their own school, LEA representatives or co-optees. So remember that you could have three or even four elected staff even in a governing body of twelve, and at least one of these has to be a support staff member. So your caretaker could stand for election. Whoever wins will have far more status, through speaking for others, if he or she is elected, and the head will have to accept this. (It isn't his choice!) If you went a bit above twelve you could have a better balance and ample provision for staff and co-optees, but remember you choose co-optees because of the perspective they bring for the school's benefit, not because they 'expect it'.

By the way, you could make your caretaker an associate member of appropriate committees, e.g. premises, if you wish. These members can have voting rights if the governing body so decides, as long as they are outnumbered at the meeting concerned by governor members, and in any case can join usefully in discussion.

What can we do about passenger governors?

The workload for governors is heavy, but most of us know it's a worthwhile job and enjoy it. It does annoy me, though, when several colleagues are clearly living in the past and make no effort to keep up to date, resist doing anything that looks like real work, and go through meetings with a constant muttering of congratulations to the school on this and commiserations on the other, all meaningless. It is as though they are still operating in the days when being a governor was just a hobby and you had no real say in anything, but felt vaguely important. How can we deal with this?

Answer

Yes, there are still governors around like the ones you describe. In any period of change there will be some dinosaurs. The quality and commitment of new entrants are now very high indeed, and many of these feel as you do about those who don't pull their weight. (Don't be too hard, though, on the mumbled niceties – they may be genuine if a little embarrassed, and real praise and sympathy have a place.) You ask what we can do. We can first make sure that when we encourage people to put themselves forward we don't, in our anxiety to avoid putting them off, say that it's just one meeting a term and the harvest festival. That's a con. What's more it won't deliver the goods, and it is far better to tell them that it needs time and commitment and that you all contribute. Do remember to say, though, that they will never, in the best possible sense, be the same again, and that it is addictively interesting.

But above all governors need to build a framework of clear expectations of each other, which will, I assure you, change things. When you go into a governing body which has this, you can't possibly miss it. It may drive away a few who can't meet the expectations, but those who learn how to do so will be grateful to you because they are no longer outsiders. No need to lecture or scold, simply convey what you expect as a group in everything you do. Expectations are the key to defining, maintaining and enriching a relationship. Refer to them when you review committee membership (now legally required at least once a year). Make sure you expect everyone to be on at least one committee. Show what you expect by the serious way you look at apologies for absence – remember you need to know the reasons, and don't be afraid to say if you think they aren't good enough. Involve governors in a plan for any recurring duties and your system (and you *must* have one) for expecting of every governor a minimum contact with the school at work.

Develop good meeting habits – give individuals an issue to research and present now and then, go round the table for comments on really important decisions, bring individuals into discussions, and make it clear that everybody is expected to go to training. When members fail to do what they've undertaken through these systems to do, NOTICE IT. A little tough love is good for everybody. It involves a totally different conception of what 'voluntary' means. Too often it is an excuse for all the ways in which we fall short. The fact that we can leave when we like, and be replaced by someone really caring and hard-working, should be seen instead as a very powerful reason for the highest standards. Only this can make being a school governor a proud calling.

> Day by day you can work to make school a friendly place, a fair place and a place which conveys good messages.

Do we really have to have committees?

Call me a heretic, but I think committees make work and can be divisive. I am chairman in a small school, we meet twice a term, and get all the work done comfortably. I see the head weekly every Monday morning, and she is very efficient and ready with questions and problems. She and I prepare well for every meeting and so get through the business briskly. It seems very artificial to divide our small manpower into four or five groups in the hope that it will somehow make work disappear, just for the sake of saying we have committees. I have heard other chairs say they end up having the same discussion twice on everything.

Answer

The short answer is that we aren't *required* to have committees. And of course I agree that we shouldn't let them proliferate for the sake of it. Having said that, I can't imagine a governing body with no committees doing all it should and involving all members democratically, with the load of business to be dealt with these days, even in a small school. Am I right in suspecting that your detailed work is largely done in your weekly meetings with the head, and that when you say 'she and I prepare well for every meeting' this may mean agreeing how to present issues in a way which provokes the minimum debate? I know this goes on, that it is relatively easy for a couple of intelligent people to do and can be quite addictive. But if matters are accepted as *faits accomplis* or go through on the nod, this may be because members don't understand them well enough to know what to ask. This is dangerous and doesn't make for good team spirit. Also, decisions thus made may not be robust and could backfire if something goes wrong and exposes their real complexity.

It is natural for governors to want to ask questions. It is unnatural for a group of assorted people to make a decision without debate. I agree you don't want to have the full debate on every subject in the governing body. Hence committees, and a really well-managed governing body will be democratic but still not allow the same discussion to take place twice. Committees with a clear remit, involving a spread of all interests, and well managed, can produce a better quality of work. Firstly they enable individuals to participate more fully in a few subject areas. Secondly they make it possible to discuss issues in more detail and depth and either deal with them (if they are delegated) or prepare them for decision. Thirdly, if they do give all governors some involvement, they can be the very opposite of divisive, especially if they are open, i.e. welcome any other governors as non-voting participants. This good practice makes individuals less prone to re-run issues at the main meetings – indeed the chair can legitimately stop them if they try. It also reduces suspicions about decisions being made by too few members.

In all my experience, when a matter is discussed for the first time in full meetings there is a real risk of power resting with too few. Firstly time is short, and thoughtful governors hesitate to hold things up even if they have a burning question. This is especially likely if, because they haven't enough detail, they are unsure what they want to ask and yet uneasy about the way things are shaping. Secondly diffident governors may find it hard to ask questions and contribute at all in a larger group. Thirdly if such a system is apparently working well – 'well-managed' as you put it – this may well be because a lot of the real discussion has taken place outside the meeting, and even the suspicion that this is so can be very divisive and demoralising.

Chair's correspondence

I know our chairman gets lots of letters addressed to him personally which the rest of us never see. Occasionally one of us will bump into a parent who refers to an approach made to the chairman and clearly thinks we are all involved. It is embarrassing, especially if the parent says the chairman hasn't replied or has sent an unhelpful or even a dismissive reply. What is the proper practice please?

Answer

The chair's role is to guide the governing body in its strategic role, to see that its business is efficiently conducted with all members able to participate, to provide team leadership, to convey agreed policies and to represent it on formal occasions. It is not to speak for us on matters we haven't made decisions on. But in reality it is normally quite impracticable and unnecessary for every letter sent to the chair to be referred to the whole governing body for an answer, and what's more we should probably complain, judging from the volume of letters our chair receives. If a correspondent asks for views on an important matter which hasn't ever been discussed by the governing body, the chair should acknowledge it and promise a reply when the question has been considered. If it is something on which the governors already have an agreed policy, a reply can probably be sent without further reference unless the governors' decision was too long ago or has been overtaken by events. Some letters may be of trivial importance, others not governors' concerns at all. The task requires a degree of judgement and we may have to forgive the odd innocent lapse. But a chair who regularly takes too much on himself or herself is dangerous. I would be very concerned about a chair who was dismissive or dilatory in replying to a parent or who expressed a view on an important matter they had never discussed. At the meeting a good chair should circulate a list of letters received, with action taken and relevant dates, since the last meeting, and the complete file should be on the table for any interested governor to see.

A local 'somebody' causing mayhem

We have a self-appointed community leader – do you know them? She has a number of roles of various kinds, on the committee of the Residents' Association, Neighbourhood Watch, Lower Lottersley Against Litter, professional objector to all planning applications. She has a very loud voice, with which she tries to discipline our pupils around the neighbourhood, she speaks disparagingly of the school in her committees, in letters to the press and in objections to our planning applications. It is a high-achieving school in a very mixed area. How can we deal with her?

Answer

Linda Snell to the life in fact, for 'Archers' fans. I think many neighbourhoods have one, in fact. What's more, even the most well-run and successful schools find that their relatively small antisocial elements are their most visible advertisement, while all the well-behaved, high-achieving students hurry along at 4.00 pm to their good mums and their homework. If it is any consolation, these self-appointed leaders often end up killing off any enterprise they *do* support.

I won't suggest you try to co-opt this lady as a governor – that would be too cruel, though ownership of problems does lead to an amazing change of perspective sometimes. What perhaps you can do is to see that you send her details of any special achievements, and also make sure that the school takes great care to maintain its profile in the local paper by informing them about its academic and sporting achievements, the destinations of its leavers, any good deeds or community enterprises involving its students. This is hard work and time-consuming, because there's a high wastage rate, but it does pay off in time. Maybe a governor or interested parent could help a staff member with this. Remember to make it easy for the newspaper staff by virtually drafting the piece and even a catchy headline, keeping it short and sending a photograph if possible. And pull all the stops out in defending any planning development which she is contesting!

You might ask the lady to honour your play or concert or presentation of records of achievement with her presence, even to plant your tree. Your students might even donate the proceeds of one of their sponsored events to a favourite charity of hers, provided it is one they agree with. This may seem to you like rewarding a villain, but she cares for the community in her own way. Remember too that people like her are as strong in advocacy as they are stern in condemnation, if you can turn them round.

> A subject attachment gives a 'window' on the school through which an individual governor can become familiar with how children learn. This is governor training rather than performance monitoring.

Absence from a meeting – is an apology enough?

One of our governors is absent on the slightest pretext, though he always apologises. He says this protects him from the six-months non-attendance penalty? Is this right?

Answer

Not automatically. It is your responsibility as a body to say whether you accept the apology and you should take this seriously, because without approval the absence counts for possible removal. For example, I would rate the closure of your nearest exit from the M25 that evening above an unexpected gift of two theatre tickets. You must also commit yourselves now and then as a group to a variety of things you consider important, like giving priority to governor commitments in your lives. I believe explicit expectations transform a governing body.

A governor's objection to specialist status

I am head of a thriving comprehensive. Although fully subscribed we are in a very competitive situation and can't afford to slacken our efforts at all – there are several equally robust schools within reasonable distance. We have good relationships with them all and the rivalry is friendly, but we all have to look to our position in the popularity stakes. The question of specialist status came up last term and our staff and most of our governors understand the issues and totally support our making a bid. So with all the other schools we are steaming ahead. We have one parent governor, however, who has strong moral objections to the idea and thinks it incompatible with the comprehensive principle and neighbourhood schools. His was the only vote against, but he won't give up. He makes fiery speeches and does everything he can to influence others, including parents, and I feel almost sabotaged. Have you any advice?

Answer

I sympathise very much in the sense that I know this process requires enormous effort and singlemindedness and a head needs to feel supported. But I also know that very many governors who feel strongly about comprehensive education have been through the same kind of turmoil as your rebel, and that is no picnic either. Some keep quiet and some resign. Many have also had the same feelings about private finance initiatives. I do not mean I would support such a governor staying in office and doing everything he or she can to undermine the majority will. Schools really are under tremendous pressure to apply for specialist status now that it is in effect open to all, and I sympathise with a head in your situation who fears that the school could be left behind. Your staff and most governors clearly understand that.

How has your chair reacted? Has he or she spoken to the governor concerned and emphasised that, while his views are respected by all, it is wrong to undermine what the majority have legally and freely decided, especially when it is too late to turn back? It is just not fair to those who have to prepare the case, because we all know what a tremendous strain that is on key staff. Schools face many difficult choices today and lots of governors feel that on one or other their school is taking the wrong direction, but we knew when we took the role on that majority opinion was the foundation of our work. Having done our best to influence colleagues beforehand, we should accept it once the deed is done, and either resign or drop the subject.

But when every form of persuasive influence has failed, I fear you have to live with it. It is true that we are now able to suspend a governor for serious misdemeanours, but although I consider public and persistent opposition to the will of the majority to be serious, I would still not advocate it in a matter of conscience like this. Anyway, I doubt whether suspension ever solves anything.

I hope you will get adequate help with preparing the bid, if only by delegating some less pressing tasks temporarily. Even without the problem you have, this, with its associated fund-raising, is an exceptionally time-consuming task, and I have heard heads say that it is all too easy to lose ground on other fronts. You need all the support you can get.

> We don't tell teachers how to teach and whom to put in detention. We discover what factors within our control can improve the conditions in which teaching takes place.

What can a staff governor take part in?

I represent the non-teaching staff on the governing body. As I manage the general office I am quite involved with the head and I fancy she is somewhat uneasy with my being a governor. We always had a governor in for interviewing candidates for teaching posts before the government stopped this involvement, and very often at short notice it was hard to get one in working hours. Under the old head I used to step in if ever we were stuck, easier for me than a teacher governor as I could always catch up my work by staying on a bit later – not like having to leave a class. Our new lady wouldn't allow this because I had no teaching experience. She also says I mustn't talk to the junior staff about what goes on at governors' meetings or bring problems from people like grounds and kitchen staff. Funnily enough, she is quite happy for me to fill a gap on a permanent exclusion appeal, indeed seems to encourage it. I am confused and would welcome guidance.

Answer

Funnily enough, the only duty I have doubts about among those you listed is the one your head is happy about. I have a great deal of evidence that some heads are uneasy about support staff governors. I don't altogether understand it, but perhaps they are bothered about the possibility of someone much less committed to the school and involved in its intimate affairs than you are – a grounds or kitchen worker say – knowing too much about its problems. Even that is absurd, because apart from classified items anyone can legally come in from the street and see governors' documents. I see no objection at all to your participating in teacher appointments when that was accepted as a proper involvement of the governors – indeed I'm sure your experience of the school equipped you especially well. After all, most parent, LEA, foundation and co-opted governors are not teachers either. I do have slightly more concern about appeals against exclusion because you will know a great deal about the students concerned and hear a lot of teacher talk, and, like the head, have understandably strong motives for getting any familiar disrupters out. But even here I can find nothing to forbid it other than the general phrase about circumstances which 'cast doubt on your ability to be impartial'. Your relationship with other non-teaching staff is no different from a parent governor's with parents or a teacher's with teaching staff. You are their representative (not a delegate – you still have to make up your own mind about the line you take, even if you faithfully convey their views) and should always be watchful for any issues that come up which may affect them or interest them. It is in fact your duty to watch their interests in any general matters that come before governors, keep them informed and consult if necessary, and take opinions back, though always remembering that the education of the children is the aim of it all. I say this last because sometimes support staff working outside the main school community do tend to bring up problems affecting their working lives, rotas, duties, relations with supervisors, etc., which are not appropriate to normal governors' business and should be taken up with their line manager, union, or in the last resort through a grievance procedure.

I hope this helps. I'm sure you will be a great asset to the governing body with your knowledge of all aspects of school management. Good luck.

Can we average infant class sizes to comply with the law?

Ours is a C of E aided primary school and I am on the admissions committee. We have applied the points system that operates for Reception class and have offered places to 30 pupils for September 2003. These have all been taken up. Appeals went before an independent appeals committee who agreed that we had applied the criteria correctly and so had to turn them all down. One child, however, was thought by at least one member of the committee to be a particularly deserving case. As class sizes are limited to 30, our hands might seem to be tied, though we should like to take the child. We do, however, only have 28 pupils in Year 1. As the average in the department would still only be 30 can we allocate the two places to Reception? Our LEA has allowed other schools to average the numbers in the classes restricted by law to 30, and so take extra children into Reception. Each class has a qualified teacher and a classroom assistant and we have the money to appoint a floating teacher to the school and may do so anyway.

Answer

I am afraid that legally 'class' means a class, not an average size in the department, and despite the apparent willingness of your LEA to condone this averaging, I can only advise that you cannot take an extra child (or two) in Reception. Even if it were legal, I think a concession in your circumstances might cause you more trouble than it was worth in the long run. With a school as oversubscribed as yours, parents will be anxiously watching what happens and you might find it more difficult – certainly less pleasant – to hold the line in future. The most you can do is put the child on the waiting list – that is, if there is no scope for 'promoting' one of the 30 to Year 1 on some wholly defensible ground such as having been in a Reception class some time somewhere else or being considerably older. This would almost certainly cause a lot of fuss too. I'm afraid the option of having a floating teacher for the whole school makes no legal difference, though it is clearly a great asset. Besides, even if you were allowed to have an over-large class it would have to move through the school and reduce flexibility to take newcomers to the area at all stages.

Interestingly I had a query the same day from another part of the country where an independent appeal tribunal had allowed an appeal which would have put the class-size above the legal maximum, despite the fact that the government gave a very strong warning to appeal committees not to make decisions which would take the infant classes concerned over the limit. The LEA here was not condoning any concessions, and the governors of the school affected were very worried about having to solve their problem by a radical reorganisation of how the pupils in the two youngest classes were grouped and taught, which parents might well dislike, however interestingly and thoughtfully it was done. At least your appeals committee did not make it impossible for you to refuse this extra child.

> Those we find easy to talk to are often not the same as those who need to be listened to.

Our chair hustles us through the meeting

We have a business-like chair so I suppose we are lucky. He prepares well for the meeting, times every item, sets out the options, and on every agenda item makes a proposal for our agreement. But he rattles through at such a pace that most would feel very conspicuous if they asked a question, voiced a doubt or, heaven forbid, disagreed. The result is that we end up feeling 'used', or even wondering if we have done the right thing. Without being ungrateful, how can we get more participation?

Answer

There's nothing wrong with preparing well, timing the items and setting out clear options. But there is something very wrong with leaving members feeling excluded, not just because it is damaging to relationships but because, more formally, our responsibility is corporate and shared ownership of the outcomes must be genuine. The chair shouldn't be the only one preparing for the meeting. Are you relying on him too much? A bit of knowledge is great for one's confidence and makes it possible to ask questions and contribute. Do you have effective committees? These, especially if open to non-members as visitors, should provide a place for a good number to dig a little deeper into issues and sort out options.

Timing of items in a rough and ready way does ensure that you get through the agenda, are disciplined in discussion, and leave enough time for really major items. But the timetable should always be put forward for general agreement at the outset, and if anyone feels the proportions are wrong he or she must say so. During the meeting you must all be brave enough to slow down the pace if you genuinely feel that a subject has not been explored enough. There may be a case for saying: 'Please could we discuss that a bit?' 'Are those the only possibilities?' or 'Can we go round the table to ensure everybody is happy with that?' This last in my experience can sometimes change the outcome. I think you will find that these techniques do the trick. If not, you may have to be more direct, or even contemplate a change.

> I never cease to be surprised by how many people's mental image of leadership is 'out in front' or 'up at the top' when in a school it's so clearly being at the centre, relating appropriately and wisely to a series of overlapping circles of parents, staff, governors.

Nobody will take a lead

We have a good lot of governors, but none with much confidence. It is hard to get anyone to be chair, and when we do there is no leadership. As head I am at a loss.

Answer

This question and the last came up on the same day. It's a big step from being a good team member to being a leader. You may have to 'nurse' a volunteer through preparing for the meeting for a while – but know when to let go. Let the vice-chair share the tasks, let individual members present some items, or use teachers to introduce a subject where the item is suitable. Make it clear you are looking for a team builder, not a figurehead. Share the burden of incidental chair duties by introducing a system of duty governor for each month, involving taking on any ceremonial items that month, like welcoming the important visitor. You will have a bigger choice for chair if you make it clear that he or she will have widespread support and will not have to carry the whole burden alone. Just put all your effort into making the job do-able at first. I think this is your best hope, and it may make for a better functioning governing body in the end than the surfeit of Very-Important types which at the moment may seem your unattainable dream.

Everything is sewn up

Becoming a governor in a new area since moving house has been a culture shock. I was used to governing bodies being open to free expression of opinion and with no power games. Now I am in an area where one party has been in control a long time, and everything is sewn up as though the 80s and 90s had never happened. The chair is a councillor and has been chair many years. His supporters chair key committees, and nobody dares challenge them. The chair and head fix the agenda and the way it will be handled, and everything is rushed through following long pre-meetings. The head is used to it and I have no idea whether he approves of it or not; I suspect it makes for an easy life. 'Chair's action' still occupies much of the time, we hardly ever vote, and everyone seems mesmerised. I'm sure you are all too familiar with it.

Answer

I am indeed. I too have lived in both kinds of culture, and those governors who have never experienced your present environment can't believe it. It must be hard for a newcomer to break in, even one who knows it isn't what was intended. But remember your LEA members are a minority, though their influence may extend beyond their numbers. In theory the rest can change things but I know how hard it is. Under new regulations (2003) *members* of the LEA cannot be co-optees, which might help.

The head is a key player, and his acceptance reflects years of conditioning. One day, when the party line doesn't suit him, he will find he's lost his authority. Someone needs to tell him how things are done elsewhere and give examples of how compliance could damage him.

Remember we elect our chair and if no one else stands no one else can be elected. Obvious but important. Committees must also be reviewed annually and the membership again elected. Your autumn meeting sews it up for whatever period you decide between one and four years. That is also the time to review your procedures – use it. The whole governing body is responsible for how the agenda is made up and must ensure that the process is open. The chair as an individual has in education law no power, except in an emergency, narrowly defined (a fire or flood), and even then only if it is an action which can legally be delegated. You can, of course, delegate many decisions to your chair, but you don't have to. Set out, the rest of you, exactly how you want things done. Things like a parent governor in every important process and teacher governors in an active role. A rota or duty period for seeing the school at work. You all decide on that.

At meetings challenge everything that seems to have been agreed in advance. Get used to saying 'Could we all discuss that?' and 'Could we go round the table and make sure no one has a problem accepting this?' Ask if there is a record of any meetings at which matters appear to have been discussed outside the governing body. Watch out particularly for any consultations on exclusions or teacher appointments and promotions, which could backfire if settled improperly. Ask your head to flag up future issues in his report to you as well as past events – then you can plan your involvement. When you toughen your stance it will make him think, and perhaps realise which side his bread is buttered. It's hard work, but without it you are all puppets.

> If every time a school got a new head ... the changeover was seen as an opportunity to develop the governing body rather than display how clever you can be at evading it, what a lot of good energy would be released.

Can we lay down our own procedures?

Can a governing body make rules for itself to ensure decent behaviour and efficiency? We would, for instance, like to restrict meeting length, and include that no governor should speak for more than five minutes (we have a few windbags). We'd include things like not interrupting, sharing the work, keeping everything confidential, observing a rota for visits. We'd like to rule that the head has the final say in anything to do with the running of the school, delegate far more decisions to the chair, head or a committee, and fix our own quorums. We would also like to restrict teacher and staff governors to matters raised by those who voted them in, as ours have a tendency to make long contributions on everything, not just their group. The head would also like them to clear any contributions with him in advance.

Answer

This is a tricky one. Codes of practice are notoriously controversial, as is shown by the difficulty the DfES once had in several attempts to get one agreed for governors. Your letter shows why. Too many prohibitions kill positive feelings about the job and might attract the wrong sort of volunteers. And while there is no reason why a governing body should not adopt rules of its own, provided – and it is a vital proviso – they don't conflict with any legal requirement, even then great care is needed. Your very mixed list contains things which *do* directly conflict and must be avoided. For instance, although most decisions can now be delegated to a committee and many to an individual, the governing body should remain free to decide this for each responsibility or decision as it arises, and should observe the statutory exclusions. And quorum is fixed legally at 50% for every decision, though governors may decide on quorums for committees (subject to a minimum of three governors). You can't give the head 'the last word' on a loosely defined range of subjects. Governors should of course keep clear of day-by-day operational decisions, but many things 'to do with the running of the school' are part of the framework of policies and principles which is our strategic responsibility. You can't restrict teacher and staff governors to 'constituency' matters: they are full governors sharing equal responsibility for the work as a whole, and in fact it would be quite wrong for them to make their contribution too narrow. Nor is it fair that they should be singled out to clear their contributions with the head in advance. We are free and equal contributors, and anything which narrows a governor's scope impoverishes the governing body. Some heads do themselves, as managers, try to impose such conditions on staff but it is not good practice. Finally, all governors' business, if not *classified* confidential, is intended to be open: your rules must not be more restrictive, though we may need to remind ourselves to report responsibly, not highlighting the role of individuals or being disloyal.

What's left? Well, I believe governors should express their high expectations of each other in agreed team-working arrangements, positive things like attendance, punctuality, sharing the work, visiting rotas, going to training, being loyal and accepting corporate responsibility. I'm less enthusiastic about restrictive provisions – keeping contributions to five minutes, for instance. You don't want to turn people away. As for limiting office-holders' terms of service, we now have to decide ourselves anyway whether to elect chair and vice-chair for one, two, three or four years. I think it is a pity to tie our own hands more than this – people and school circumstances change. Finally and most important, any rules should express the will of all of you, not a few wishing to put restraints on others.

Our meetings are dominated by two or three

I am new but keen. The way our meetings are run makes it impossible to break in. Only a few senior governors ever speak, and I don't know whether others are shy, uninterested, or haven't read the papers. I'm not quite brave enough to assert myself.

Answer

We really handle induction badly. At least make up your mind now that the next new governor has a *planned* and civilised introduction to the job. Probably no new governor has been properly welcomed for years. Meanwhile, why don't you ask the most promising of the silent governors what s/he thinks is the problem? Ask your chair too – it's his or her responsibility to secure participation. Don't forget we are obliged to review committee membership every year: silent members shouldn't find it so easy to coast along in a small group. But don't waste the once-in-a-lifetime opportunity of being new. That's when you can say 'Please could we all discuss that?' or 'Please can we go round the table and just make sure everyone is happy before we make that decision?' without people thinking you are winding them up. You might even suggest your governing body starts asking different members to introduce a suitable item now and then, preparing the ground by reading up the history and suggesting ways forward. If you've been motivated to write to me you can surely find ways to break up this self-appointed A team.

Please explain all these changes*

There's a lot I don't understand about the rules we shall be working under in this new school year. For instance I am a chair who has been in office far too long, and a year ago I was determined it was my last. Then our head got a job in a bigger school and my colleagues begged me to stay until we'd made an appointment. Our new head started this term and now they want me to stay through his first term at least to manage a proper handover. Does this mean I have to serve another four years? Also it seems we have decisions to make about how many representatives of each category we want, and I wouldn't know where to start. The size and proportions have always worked pretty well and I wouldn't want to reduce any group. Have you any advice to give? As for rules, I feel that a lot of very sensible rules have been revoked without replacement. The general impression is that we have to be much brisker and delegate everything, which could be tricky with a new head and new structure. Ours is an LEA co-ed comprehensive with just short of a thousand pupils 11 to 16.

(* September 2003, but relevant for two or three years)

Answer

I think you misunderstand the election rules. A chair can be elected, by agreement, for one, two, three or four years. Even then you can resign when ready and your governing body again decides on the term of office.

Now size, on which you can take your time. At present you have twenty governors including the head, so you can only move down in size – twenty is the maximum allowed. You can stay with that if you want to. You now have six parent governors, and the law says at least one third, i.e. seven in your case, at all times *must* be parents, so you'd need one more if you kept to twenty. You have four staff, including the head. That's well within the maximum of one third, and you could have one more if you wanted to reduce the five LEA and five co-optees you have now to four each (the new minima). You have to lose one anyway to accommodate the extra parent, which would still leave a pretty good balance of elected members from the school and others. Talk about this now and return to it at intervals in the light of how your meetings go – are you too many for effective discussion, has everyone been able to have a say, does the balance feel right, have you enough or more than enough for all the jobs? In smaller governing bodies I would say start by deciding how many you want for the staff group (no more than one third including the head) and look at the balance from there. You can only have a support staff member if you have at least three in all, and even then some think one teacher is too little.

I agree that some good rules have been dropped. But if there is something missing that you thought was good practice you can adopt it informally, if and as long as all agree, though it won't have the protection of law. You can adopt new working rules too, if and as long as you all think them necessary. For instance, I'd like to see an agreement that any three governors have a right to put an item on the agenda – after all, they can call a special meeting! The remaining *legal* changes are new permissive rules, which do allow many opportunities for delegating decisions to an individual or a committee. But remember you only delegate when a majority of you desire it, except for staff appointments and dismissals below deputy which must be delegated to the head. Do begin talking about these important things soon and return to them when they have simmered a bit.

> The majority of governors who ask me questions are still concerned with a handful of unchangeables – their role and its limits, their problems in representing particular interest groups, their relations with the head teacher and staff, the efficiency of their working arrangements and the interplay of different interests within the governing body.

How can we have our caretaker and school secretary and two teachers on the governing body?

Before 1998 we used to save a co-opted place for our schoolkeeper, but of course since then it has not been possible, and he was elected as a staff representative in 2000. Now we shall have to sacrifice the non-teaching place, as his service finishes this term, because we all think we must have two teachers and the head under our new constitution, and being a very small school that means no support staff. We would in any case like to have our school secretary rather than the caretaker (can we specify this?), though we'd really like them both. The government doesn't seem to realise that these support staff are especially important members of the team in a very small school. Can we now co-opt again?

Answer

Any new staff governor on governing bodies has to be elected (no co-options of any full-time employees of the school), and election of a staff governor must be by and from *all* the non-teaching staff, so what you suggest isn't possible. You must not try to influence the outcome. Do you really need two teacher governors in such a very small school? If so, you seem to have overlooked the fact that you can move to a larger governing body if you want. Any number over twelve will accommodate four staff places and the minimum of four parents, with two LEA and two co-opted. If the school secretary were elected you could make the caretaker an associate member of relevant committees if you wished, even with voting rights (as long as there were always a majority of full governors present). It doesn't have the same status as an elected representative, but you would benefit from his point of view and experience.

Should we monitor staff sickness absence?

Our LEA has issued a paper about teacher absence rates and suggested that schools monitor these with a view to tightening up on unwarranted sick leave. As you can imagine, this has caused ill-feeling among school staffs, and in the school where I am chair of governors the hard-working teachers feel it to be an outrageous implication. The LEA says our rates are high compared with our neighbours'. Do you think it reasonable that we should review them, given the hurtful implication?

Answer

I don't know how widespread the practice is but I think you will find that it is growing. After all, we now look carefully at *pupil* attendance and try to raise standards, with no reflection on the large number of pupils who attend regularly and are conscientious about taking time off, just as most teachers are. I know this is a highly sensitive issue with teachers and that the overwhelming majority are outstandingly responsible, and indeed often keep working when they are under par, to the detriment of their general health. They do have good holidays, but, unlike many professions, can't take them in the form of the odd day's leave when they feel it would benefit their health, and they hate putting burdens on their colleagues. This can have the effect of prolonging and exacerbating health problems through trying to keep going. One must also point out that teaching *is* stressful and that working closely with large numbers of children exposes teachers to high infection risks.

Having said all this, I must add that most employers routinely analyse sickness absence and investigate further where the analysis reveals problems. Many do so, not in a punitive spirit, but wishing firstly to help any staff who may have special difficulties, and secondly to ensure that all staff observe the same standards when deciding whether time off is justified. In schools it is of course local management, and especially the fact that tight budgets highlight the cost of supply cover, which has put sick leave under the microscope.

So yes, I do think it is reasonable to keep rates of sickness absence under review, with the proviso that those who do it should be positive in their motives, sensitive, aware of how stressful teaching can be, sympathetic to staff who have particular problems, and flexible in taking account of any chronic ailments, accidents or long investigative processes which make some figures look worse than they are. A short interview with a line manager following return from sick leave seems also to be becoming more common to pick up any problems the teacher may have. I know that some employers are actually hard on staff who have taken more days off sick than they think acceptable. I would hate to think that education was going down that road, or indeed that it was not to remain among the best employers in its care for staff welfare. I do, on the other hand, believe that a certain amount of watchfulness is our duty when we are looking after the school's money, and that the very existence of a check may influence the tiny minority who may need it.

I leave till last, for greater emphasis, one of the most important justifications on the positive side, a reminder that staff sickness rates can occasionally be a reflection of the general state of morale in the school – or even a particular department – that special difficulties in its catchment area, budget, staff ratios and workloads may cause, and the quality of management and care. Sickness absence rates, properly analysed, could thus also be a valuable diagnostic aid.

Governors can only be effective at a strategic level and are not there to check up on what goes on in the classroom, the playground or the office.

Is a work-related curriculum divisive?

As a governor I am fighting with my feelings. It is with regard to separating off less able students in our comprehensive for work experience part-time. I had a poor background in the Northeast a long way from where I now live, and I know from my parents how schooling after 14 (grandparents even earlier, when it was the shipyards or 'service') was a privilege as well as escaping from poor jobs. Where I am now there is more opportunity and plenty of work of all kinds, but I thought the national curriculum would give the same chances to everybody. Not just the three Rs but science and languages and music and everything. Are we slipping back? I find I am putting my hand up for quite a few things that worry me nowadays, but this is the one I find hardest. Someone once told me when you came here to our conference that you had the same sort of background as me, and I wonder if you will understand this.

Answer

Yes, indeed I did, except for us it was the mines or domestic service, and I understand just what you are saying. I also know we all 'put our hands up' for things that worry us sometimes, because we don't always choose the alternatives, and in the end we can only do the best available for our school. On the question you raise I confess I have had the same feelings about the broad curriculum, but they have been changed by experience in our own school. I can see for myself that struggling with too heavy a curriculum diet can be dispiriting and isolating rather than equalising, especially in a school with a very wide ability range which does its best to give every child some experience of success. (I remember my father quoting his old headmaster who said every child needed to be good at something and if you didn't give it to them they might well choose spitting!) I have sat on your letter a week or so because of these feelings, but this is the week I went to the school to see an exhibition by, and talk to, the students who are on extended work experience, and I can only say that their self-confidence is amazing, and the staff say the remarkable thing is not only their pride in doing something successful, but their behaviour and improvement in coping with the school subjects.

There are conditions that must be satisfied, of course. All students must have work experience, as well as the group who have it earlier and more extensively. The staff must believe in the programme and have respect for all the young people. Their achievement, whatever it is, must not be second best in anyone's eyes, and placings must be monitored carefully. The students must be recognised – our school established new prizes for the best of them this year. They must be supported to a degree which enables all to leave with some GCSEs as well. The

112

curriculum doors must remain open to any talent whatever. And for me, above all there must be the fullest opportunities in the school to experience and perhaps to excel in a wide variety of sports, in drama, music and art, and with distinction in any of these given as much prominence as exam results.

> It's so much easier to deal with ordinary human forgetfulness if you have something written down that you all agreed to.

Where did we go wrong last year?

I remember your saying the first meeting in the autumn was a vital one because you could put your mistakes right with less pain, but I'm afraid I was very smug and dismissive. 'That isn't our problem,' I said. But looking back, I can truly say this was a dreadful year. The 'team' was a shambles. A few new governors got the wrong ideas and upset head and staff by interfering in classroom matters – teaching styles, homework, punishment. Some older governors had lost their enthusiasm and were not taking their share of duties, visiting or contributing, while a few assumed self-appointed leadership roles. How can things go so wrong when you think you are old hands? Say it again, please.

Answer

Many must think I've said it too often. But when you've been round the track a few times you realise that without a maintenance plan a governing body is like an old house: something is always leaking, creaking or falling apart. The point about the autumn term is that we've all had a break, bad habits no longer have name tags on them, and certain things we have to do focus the mind on clearing clutter and mending leaks.

First there's the chair. If you've got a great chair, a team-builder rather than a figurehead, be grateful. But if there was too much 'I'll have a word', 'The head and I thought...', 'Are we all agreed then?', remember if you do nothing you'll get him or her again. We have for some time been encouraged to nominate in advance in time for the agenda, and although from September 2003 we have been free to organise the election as we like, it's still wise to think ahead because if there isn't another offer you'll get the same one elected – and you did it yourselves!

This is the best time to look at your committees. Make sure that their chairs, however good, haven't become a caucus group. If they are superb, be grateful, but remember that a governing body must grow and develop, and 'hope long deferred maketh the heart sick'. You may be able to freshen the mix and create new opportunities by splitting large and busy committees by subject or creating some task groups.

This is the time, too, to remind yourself about all sorts of tasks, and especially things that had gone awry but were too personalised to correct at the time. Very basic things, like remembering that an individual governor has no power and that all governors must focus on the big picture and leave daily management to those whose job it is. That decisions are made together and all are loyal to them. How to behave when visiting the school, being discreet about things you pick up about staff and children through your privileged access, representing others without being their mouthpiece. What policies need updating and how agreed ones are stored. How you can make sure you get early warning of matters likely to need your attention in the near future, so that you don't just nod them through. Time to establish good procedures and principles for sharing work and responsibility: rotas for routine tasks like attending parents' meetings; attachments to subjects, classes or a duty month; looking after new colleagues. It's so much easier to deal with ordinary human forgetfulness if you have something written down that you all agreed to. We all look back now and then on a year when things fell apart, but only rarely are we denied another chance.

How much involvement?

You are always insistent that every governor should be prepared to spend some time in the school when it is working and also on becoming familiar with the legal requirements. Up to a point I agree with this, but I would like to say that it can be a form of privilege to have that sort of time and that sort of ability, and that we do need governors who are more representative of ordinary people and people outside education. I also observe from experience that sometimes those who are in this sense privileged on a governing body tend to become the A team, and that there is an unspoken assumption that nobody without a lot of time and knowledge is qualified to take over. Thus new governors with different circumstances may be marginalised. Is there something in this?

Answer

Yes, there is. I would still not budge from the belief that without some understanding of the learning process day by day we can't really make the best decisions or have a proper appreciation of teachers' skills and problems. I also know that there are some people who, because they work from home, are on flexi-time or part-time, or have enlightened employers who give governors extra leave, are in your sense privileged. But I am not talking about huge amounts of time – a

114

day a term, perhaps, over and above the routine tasks we all share, with some kind of attachment (to class or subject area or period of duty) to give it focus. It's how the time is used, not how much. As for knowledge of the rules, they are not difficult and there are many simple summaries. Their importance is just what you say – knowledge conveys privilege, and if there are some governors who sit there and think 'That doesn't sound right to me but I'd better keep quiet because I don't know where it says', they are immediately excluded from a decision they should be sharing. That's exactly why I so often say that the procedures must be understood by all if there is to be real equality on the governing body.

Having said all this, I do think that if we are not vigilant we may be encouraged to accept too strict a definition of what constitutes 'enough' knowledge and experience, so that, as you suggest, a group of governors may feel excluded from responsible positions and processes. A head who recently raised this with me called it an invisible 'tariff' for involvement, and condemned it as an unintentional perpetuation of an A team and a static committee system. That seemed to me a very thoughtful comment, which I took to heart. But those privileged by circumstances rarely mean to exploit the fact, and I believe most governors want as widespread a sharing of influence as can be achieved, and work for that. Nevertheless I am grateful for your comments which remind us all to be careful. May I say in conclusion that the most impressive governors I have met up and down the country include many who have started with no specialised knowledge or experience but with a tremendous commitment to the job and a seemingly natural empathy with schools and teachers. They tend to learn very fast, but retain a purity of understanding which you sometimes feel too much knowledge might compromise. I am with you in wanting to preserve this balance.

The governors I have met remain an inspiration which illuminates every day.

Appendix:

A guide to the changes applying from September 2003

A. Constitution

1. Changing the way governors do their work

Regulations made under the Education Act 2002 came out in the summer of 2003, and could change in many important ways the operation of governing bodies. The period of transition extends from September 2003 to July 2006, when the process should be complete, but some changes applied immediately from 1st September 2003.

2. How and why

The aim was to give governing bodies more freedom to organise their work to suit their own circumstances and styles, setting up over the three-year period (within guidelines laid down) their own new constitutions, and operating from September 2003 under new procedures based on greater delegation to the head, the chair and committees if they so wish. The new constitutional provisions on the size and composition of governing bodies are covered in Statutory Instrument 2003 No. 348 and their working rules in Statutory Instrument 2003 No. 1377. Statutory Instrument 2003 No. 1963 on governors' involvement in staff selection and dismissal is also relevant. The constitutional changes give governors a choice of size and membership, both within prescribed guidelines, and the new working procedures give them the opportunity to cut corners in their decision making. The points to emphasise are (a) that the proposals are all interrelated and their consequences should be considered as a whole before irrevocable changes are made; and (b) that although the law-makers may have hoped that all the changes leading to the streamlining of decision making would be welcomed, governing bodies are still free to choose how far they go down that road and are in many cases free to keep traditional practice.

In more detail:

3. Size

The governing body can choose its own size, between 9 and 20 members, regardless of the size of the school. The wise governing body will have looked at the membership options first, to see what size would produce for them the best balance of interests to safeguard open and democratic working.

4. Membership

As follows:

(i) community schools (including nursery and special)

(a)   at least one third parent governors

(b)   at least two, but no more than one third, staff governors, to include the head. (A place is kept for the head even if he/she decides not to be a governor.) If three or more, one must be a support staff governor, unless no one stands for election

(c)   one fifth LEA governors

(d)   one fifth or more community governors.

The governing body may also appoint up to two sponsor governors to represent benefactors, these last in addition to designated size.

(ii) foundation schools

(a)   parent and (b) staff governors, as in community schools

(c)   at least one, and not more than one fifth, LEA governors

(d)   one tenth or more community governors and

(e)   at least two, but not more than one quarter, foundation or, where the school has no foundation, partnership governors.

The governing body may also appoint up to two sponsor governors to represent benefactors, these last in addition to designated size.

(iii) voluntary controlled schools

(a)   parent, staff and LEA governors, as in community schools

(b)   community governors: one tenth or more

(c)   at least two, but no more than a quarter, foundation governors.

The governing body may also appoint up to two sponsor governors to represent benefactors, these last in addition to designated size.

(iv) voluntary aided schools

(a)   at least one elected parent governor

(b)   at least two, but not more than one third, staff governors

(c)   at least one, but no more than one tenth, LEA governors

(d)   such number of foundation governors as will outnumber the total of the other three categories by two. In this last group there must be enough current parents to bring the total of parents up to one third.

In addition, sponsor governors – up to two – may be appointed to represent benefactors, over and above the constitutional number.

Size and proportions will together make what you consider a balanced body.

B. New working rules

(i) election of chair

The big change is that a governing body can elect a chair (and vice-chair) for a fixed term between one year and four years. Previously we were required to elect annually. Some governing bodies may welcome this because they can give an ideal candidate a finite but worthwhile period of service to plan for, and it also removes the embarrassment of replacing a chair who has gone on too long. On the other hand people and circumstances change unpredictably: some chairs start with a flourish but are disappointing in the long haul, others develop with experience. Schools also go through cycles and their needs change, e.g. they might want an outgoing chair to see a new head settled or OfSTED over. Some governing bodies may therefore choose to keep their options open through a policy of electing only for one year at a time, as previously. Current chair and vice-chair must leave the meeting while the election takes place. There remains a procedure for removing chair or vice-chair from office, somewhat simpler than the former rules. The chair's responsibilities are spelled out in the accompanying guidance, and as well as ensuring the proper conduct of business, orderly meetings and a fruitful relationship with the head, he or she must ensure that all members have an equal opportunity to participate.

(ii) quorum and delegation

The new all-purpose quorum of 50% laid down is not open to choice. It used to be one third for everyday decisions and two-thirds for a range of very important ones (e.g. co-opting colleagues and delegating powers). Similarly with delegation, which previously was not allowed for a long list of important decisions like ratifying the choice of head or deputy, altering or closing the school, approving the budget or creating a wide range of statutory policies. Now almost any decision *may* be delegated to a committee and most *may* be delegated to an individual – exceptions are listed at the end of this section.

Any committee or individual exercising delegated power must report to the whole governing body on the exercise of that power. Smaller governing bodies risk placing power in a relatively small number of hands which could become an unrepresentative interest group. Do remember that, while the new quorum percentage applies whether we like it or not, the decision to delegate or not remains with the governing body. Of course we should delegate when efficiency demands it, but we can be selective. The smaller the governing body, the more careful it needs to be.

Decisions which cannot be delegated to an individual are:
alteration or discontinuance of the school; change of category of school; approval to the first formal budget plan of the financial year; the determination of admission arrangements or the admission of a particular child; school discipline policies; the exclusion of pupils; constitutional changes relating to the governing body.

(iii) committees

There are no longer any statutory committees for pupil discipline or staff dismissal, which governing bodies are now free to deal with in the more permissive context of these regulations. (On staff appointments and dismissals, however, the present regulations must be read in connection with those concerned only with staffing matters. See opposite.) Governing bodies may delegate almost all their functions to committees, giving them such powers as they wish and determining their membership, rules and terms of reference, and reviewing these matters annually. In general, membership of committees may include associate members (non-governors) but the governing body determines whether these may vote and can remove them at any time. Only associate members over 18 may vote, and then only on matters other than admissions, pupil discipline, election or appointment of governors, or the budget and financial commitments of the governing body; and the committee may exclude such members from any discussion on individual pupils or teachers. The governing body must also appoint a clerk to each committee, who may not be the head teacher. Committee chairs must be appointed annually, either by the governing body or by the committee itself – the governing body decides which. The quorum, determined by the committee, may not be less than three. The committee chair signs and approves the minutes.

(iv) appointments and staff discipline

The separate regulations on staffing matters are too long and complex to deal with fully here, but the main provisions are as follows. The *overall* responsibility of governing bodies for staff appointments and discipline, dismissal and grievance procedures remains. But (from September 2003, or at the latest in special circumstances May 2004) they will be expected to delegate the detailed selection procedure for all staff below the level of deputy to the head teacher. The governing body is no longer required to establish a standing disciplinary committee for staff, because the head teacher will also take over the discipline and dismissal of staff below deputy. It is implied that some provision for appeal will need to be made, and it will be up to governors to set this up, similarly grievance procedures. There is provision for close liaison with the LEA on delicate issues. It is significant on appointments that the governing body's overall responsibility for framing job specifications for staff is mentioned, a valuable check on fairness, especially for internal candidates. The arrangements for appointing heads and deputies remain very similar to the previous ones, involving the election of a panel whose choice must be ratified by the whole governing body. The former requirement for a pupil discipline committee as such is also dropped, and governors can deal with this within their general power to delegate particular tasks to committees.

(v) meetings

Governing bodies must meet at least three times a year, and seven days' notice must be given of a meeting, as at present. Committees (and the head teacher, whether or not a member) must also have seven days' notice from the clerk, unless the governing body has determined otherwise. A vote may only be taken in committees where a majority of those present are governors. The quorum in committee meetings will be determined by the committee, but may not be less than three members of the governing body. The head may attend any committee meetings and the governing body or the committee may approve the attendance of any other persons – i.e. it is still possible to have committees open to any governor if the governing body wishes. As at present, any member with a pecuniary interest in a matter under discussion or a partner with such an interest, or any member whose circumstances cast doubt on his or her ability to be impartial on any decision, must withdraw, but may give evidence if appropriate.

(vi) suspension of governors

The governing body may suspend for up to six months any member who is a staff member undergoing disciplinary proceedings, is being tried for a disqualifying offence, or has breached confidentiality, offended against the ethos of the school, or otherwise brought the governing body into disrepute. This is a new power, and the matter must be on the agenda. No guidance is given about what happens at the end of the period, but the governor may not be disqualified for non-attendance during that period, and may receive papers. He or she may make a statement in response but must afterwards withdraw.

C. Collaboration and federation

September 2003 also saw the publication of new regulations enabling governing bodies to co-operate more closely among themselves. These cover a range of formal collaborative relationships with other schools, including the establishment of joint committees with power to carry out certain functions. Schools may even federate under a single governing body with a view to becoming stronger and more effective than they could on their own, and more focused on common local problems. This is entirely up to governors to decide for themselves, weighing the advantages against possible loss of local accountability, some duplication of school-specific tasks, and perhaps some loss of personal commitment to, and knowledge of, one familiar school among the membership. Obviously a big decision. Because it may not as yet interest many governing bodies it is not dealt with fully here. The procedures and rules are extremely complex, and interested governing bodies should study the regulations very carefully themselves and seek help from their local governor support team.

A selection of titles from Network Educational Press

THE SCHOOL EFFECTIVENESS SERIES

Book 1: *Accelerated Learning in the Classroom* by Alistair Smith
Book 2: *Effective Learning Activities* by Chris Dickinson
Book 3: *Effective Heads of Department* by Phil Jones and Nick Sparks
Book 4: *Lessons are for Learning* by Mike Hughes
Book 5: *Effective Learning in Science* by Paul Denley and Keith Bishop
Book 6: *Raising Boys' Achievement* by Jon Pickering
Book 7: *Effective Provision for Able & Talented Children* by Barry Teare
Book 8: *Effective Careers Education & Guidance* by Andrew Edwards and Anthony Barnes
Book 9: *Best behaviour and Best behaviour FIRST AID* by Peter Relf, Rod Hirst, Jan Richardson and Georgina Youdell
Best behaviour FIRST AID (pack of five booklets)
Book 10: *The Effective School Governor* by David Marriott *(including free audio tape)*
Book 11: *Improving Personal Effectiveness for Managers in Schools* by James Johnson
Book 12: *Making Pupil Data Powerful* by Maggie Pringle and Tony Cobb
Book 13: *Closing the Learning Gap* by Mike Hughes
Book 14: *Getting Started* by Henry Leibling
Book 15: *Leading the Learning School* by Colin Weatherley
Book 16: *Adventures in Learning* by Mike Tilling
Book 17: *Strategies for Closing the Learning Gap* by Mike Hughes and Andy Vass
Book 18: *Classroom Management* by Philip Waterhouse and Chris Dickinson
Book 19: *Effective Teachers* by Tony Swainston
Book 20: *Transforming Teaching and Learning* by Colin Weatherley, Bruce Bonney, John Kerr and Jo Morrison
Book 21: *Effective Teachers in Primary Schools* by Tony Swainston

ACCELERATED LEARNING SERIES General Editor: **Alistair Smith**

Accelerated Learning – A User's Guide by Alistair Smith, Mark Lovatt & Derek Wise
Accelerated Learning in Practice by Alistair Smith
The ALPS Approach: Accelerated Learning in Primary Schools
   by Alistair Smith and Nicola Call
MapWise by Oliver Caviglioli and Ian Harris
The ALPS Approach Resource Book by Alistair Smith and Nicola Call
Creating an Accelerated Learning School by Mark Lovatt and Derek Wise
ALPS StoryMaker by Stephen Bowkett
Thinking for Learning by Mel Rockett and Simon Percival
Reaching out to all learners by Cheshire LEA
Leading Learning by Alistair Smith
Bright Sparks by Alistair Smith
Move It by Alistair Smith

ABLE AND TALENTED CHILDREN COLLECTION

Effective Resources for Able and Talented Children by Barry Teare
More Effective Resources for Able and Talented Children by Barry Teare
Challenging Resources for Able and Talented Children by Barry Teare

MODEL LEARNING

Thinking Skills & Eye Q by Oliver Caviglioli, Ian Harris and Bill Tindall
Think it–Map it! by Oliver Caviglioli and Ian Harris
Reaching out to all thinkers by Oliver Caviglioli and Ian Harris

OTHER TITLES

Basics for School Governors by Joan Sallis
The Thinking Child by Nicola Call with Sally Featherstone
The Thinking Child Resource Book by Nicola Call with Sally Featherstone
StoryMaker Catch Pack by Stephen Bowkett
Becoming Emotionally Intelligent by Catherine Corrie
That's Science! by Tim Harding
That's Maths! by Tim Harding
The Brain's Behind It by Alistair Smith
Help Your Child To Succeed by Bill Lucas and Alistair Smith
Help Your Child To Succeed – Toolkit by Bill Lucas and Alistair Smith
Tweak to Transform by Mike Hughes
Imagine That... by Stephen Bowkett
Self-Intelligence by Stephen Bowkett
Class Talk by Rosemary Sage
Lend Us Your Ears by Rosemary Sage
A World of Difference by Rosemary Sage

**For more information and ordering details, please consult our website
www.networkpress.co.uk**